COME

A teen's guide on how to pray,
have a closer relationship with God,
and experience His goodness

Cover design by Sara Young
Cover photo by Tika Cook

ISBN: 978-1-962401-85-2   1 2 3 4 5 6 7 8 9 10

Printed in the United States of America

KATHY R. GREEN

COME

*A teen's guide on how to pray,
have a closer relationship with God,
and experience His goodness*

REVISED EXPANDED EDITION

KUDU
PUBLISHING

DEDICATION

*To my granddaughter, Grace, a beautiful, kind,
thoughtful, intelligent, and gifted pray-er.*

CONTENTS

"Woe to the generation of sons who find their own censers empty of the rich incense of prayer, whose fathers have been too busy or too unbelieving to pray, and who have inexpressible perils and untold consequences for their heritage! They whose fathers and mothers have left them a wealthy legacy of prayer are very fortunate, indeed."
—E. M. Bounds[1]

TO ALL THE SONS AND DAUGHTERS:

On behalf of any adult in your life who has failed to be there for you when you needed someone most, I ask your forgiveness. May you have the courage to forgive whomever you need to. If you have ever felt unseen, unheard, unimportant, or abandoned, please know that God sees you. He sees your pain and disappointments, and He knows the cry of your heart. That is why He commissioned me to write this book. As you read its pages, I pray that you will open your heart and allow God to speak to you. At the end of each chapter, take time to *Come Closer* to God by reflecting on what you have read, answering the questions, and writing down your thoughts and feelings or whatever God speaks to your heart. I pray that your life will be filled with the rich rewards of talking to God and spending time with Him in the Secret Place.

---

1 E. M. Bounds, *E. M. Bounds on Prayer* (New Kensington, PA: Whitaker House, 1997) 13.

Then Jesus said, "Come to me, all of you who are weary and carry heavy burdens, and I will give you rest. Take my yoke upon you. Let me teach you because I am humble and gentle at heart, and you will find rest for your souls. For my yoke is easy to bear, and the burden I give you is light."
—Matthew 11:28-30 (NLT)

CHAPTER ONE

GOD IS CALLING!

Something is seriously wrong. Either adults have failed this generation's youth by not passing on a legacy of prayer, or the enemy is more powerful than we realize. Whatever the reason, somehow, an entire generation of young people seems to be moving further away from God instead of closer to Him.

Living in this technological age has made communicating with friends and family easier and faster than ever with the use of cell phones, text messaging, and social media. Take a minute to think about how much time you spend engaging in technology and on social media sites. You may not know it, but God wants you to talk to Him too! It may seem impossible to talk to God as much as you talk to your friends, but God desires the same attention and respect that you give everyone else in your life. Simply stated, He doesn't want to be ignored.

God doesn't mind us enjoying technology. In fact, He is the One who gave man the creative, brilliant, and innovative mind to create such fine instruments of communication. However, He doesn't want us to spend so much time communicating with our friends that we forget about Him. I'll go as far as to say that God is jealous. It may sound strange to mention God and jealousy in the same sentence, but the Bible describes Him as a jealous lover (James 4:5). He loves us so much, and He wants to spend time with us. God is jealous for us just like a boyfriend or girlfriend would be if the person they were dating spent more time with someone else. The Bible tells us not to have other gods before Him, and when we do, these things become idols in our lives. What's more, we were created to have relationship, fellowship, and conversation with our heavenly Father, and He must have first place in our lives.

> WE WERE CREATED TO HAVE RELATIONSHIP, FELLOWSHIP, AND CONVERSATION WITH OUR HEAVENLY FATHER, AND HE MUST HAVE FIRST PLACE IN OUR LIVES.

You may feel unseen or as if you have been forgotten, but God sees you. He has not forgotten you.

He has promised to never leave you or forsake you. In the Old Testament, there were people who complained because they felt like God had forgotten and forsaken them. And the Lord answered:

> *"Can a woman forget her nursing child that she should not have compassion on the son of her womb? Yes, they may forget, yet I will not forget*

you. Behold, I have indelibly imprinted (tattooed
a picture of) you in the palm of each of My hands."
—Isaiah 49:15-16 (AMP)

Even at this very moment God's arms are open wide, and He is calling you to come to Him. No matter what you are doing or what you have done in the past, God loves you unconditionally, and He accepts you just the way you are. God is calling you into a deeper, fuller, and richer relationship with Him—and He has more in store for you than you could ever hope for, or even imagine.

- ♦ He wants to reveal His love, goodness, kindness, and mercy to you.
- ♦ God wants to speak to you about the plans and purposes He has for your life.
- ♦ He wants to teach you how to live.
- ♦ God wants to talk to you and listen to what you have to say.
- ♦ He wants to respond to the cries of your heart and answer your prayers.

God sits on His throne in heaven watching over you just like parents enjoy watching their children playing at the park. Seeing their children happy, having fun, and enjoying life gives parents so much joy and satisfaction, and it's the same with God. He wants you happy and enjoying your life. God wants you to know Him like you would a close friend. He wants you to learn to trust Him and to be comfortable talking to Him about anything and everything going on in your life. God is concerned about the same things you're concerned about. He wants you to come to Him and talk about the things you can't tell anyone else. He wants you to be comfortable and transparent enough to discuss things with Him because it's foolish to think we can hide things from God just because we don't talk to Him about them openly. He already knows about every detail of our lives anyway.

So what's holding you back? What keeps you from spending time with God?

The devil will try anything to keep you from spending time with God. He will use things like guilt and condemnation over whatever you've done wrong, or he will try to get you to think that God is angry with you. Maybe he has told you that you have to be perfect before you can come to God. None of these things are true. The enemy knows if he can get you to believe his lies, then he can get you to spend your lifetime trying to be good enough to win God's approval and never experience the love of God or a real relationship with Him.

> ## THE TRUTH IS, GOD WANTS YOU TO COME TO HIM JUST LIKE YOU ARE.

The truth is, God wants you to come to Him just like you are. There is no one good or perfect aside from Christ because it's only through the blood of Jesus that we are made perfect in Him. Mark 10 tells of a man who came running to Jesus, knelt down, and asked him, "Good Teacher, what can I do to inherit eternal life?" And Jesus replied, "Why do you call Me good? Only God is good" (v. 18). Even Jesus didn't call Himself good—only God our heavenly Father is good and perfect. So it doesn't matter if you are "good" or "bad," God just wants you to come to Him. One time, there were some parents who tried to take their children to see Jesus so that He could put His hands on them, pray for them, and bless them. While they were approaching Jesus, His disciples tried to stop them. I'm sure His disciples thought Jesus had much more important things to take care of, like healing the sick and raising the dead. But they were wrong.

Instead of Jesus turning the children away as if they were of little or no value to Him, He used the opportunity to teach the disciples a very important lesson. He told them, "Let the little children come to Me, and do not forbid them; for of such is the kingdom of God" (Luke 18:16). In essence, what He was saying is that God's kingdom is made up of people who are childlike at heart. Not childish, but childlike—humble, pure of heart, forgiving, loving, teachable, moldable, trusting, and having faith to simply believe. Jesus also told them that "whoever doesn't receive the kingdom of God as a little child will by no means enter it" (Luke 18:17). It takes humility to come to God. Pride says, "I don't need God," but a humble person runs to Him.

Jesus called the children to come and be blessed then, and He is still calling you to come now.

COME CLOSER!

Remember, God is calling you to come to Him. He doesn't want to punish you, He wants to bless you!

What do you want God to do for you? What is God speaking to you through this chapter? Jot down your thoughts here.

_____

_____

_____

_____

_____

_____

_____

_____

_____

_____

Prayer: "Father God, forgive me for not spending time with You like I should. I know that You love me and want to bless me. Please help me to know You more closely."

CHAPTER TWO

COME AND BE HEARD

"Even if my father and mother should
desert me, You will take care of me."
—Psalm 27:10 (CEV)

Have you ever longed for someone to really talk to who won't judge you for who you are? Everyone needs someone like that. When friends and family fail to notice when you're crying out for help, God is there. He's faithful, trustworthy, and always the same. He will never let you down.

The teenage years can be the most difficult and challenging time in someone's life, but they don't have to be. These should be fun and happy years that you can look back on and laugh about and tell your children about without guilt or shame. The devil doesn't want that. He is trying to fill your teenage years with heartache and pain as a result of your poor choices or the poor choices of those around you. The enemy wants to fill your life with guilt over the mistakes you've made and make you so ashamed that you will never become the great person God has destined for you to be.

> WHEN FRIENDS AND FAMILY FAIL TO NOTICE WHEN YOU'RE CRYING OUT FOR HELP, GOD IS THERE. HE'S FAITHFUL, TRUSTWORTHY, AND ALWAYS THE SAME. HE WILL NEVER LET YOU DOWN.

The teenage years are often rough and rocky years because they are transitional. Everything is changing. A teenager is no longer a child but not yet an adult. You're in the process of discovering who you are and who you want to be one day. You're finding out who your real friends are—and those who are not your friends. You want to fit in and be a part of the "in crowd," and on top of all that, your body is changing. It's a time when feelings of loneliness set in and the desire to be with someone special. If you have a boyfriend or girlfriend, you are faced with the temptation to sin.

IS ANYONE HOME?

Now is the time when you need someone like never before, but, sadly enough, you may have no one. It seems that your generation has been forgotten. Who's really there for you when you need them most? Who's home with you before and after school? Who's there when you want someone to talk to? Does anybody really care?

You've probably heard the expression "latchkey kids." These are the children and teens who come home to an empty house after school. They are left to themselves until a parent or guardian arrives home from work. The latchkey generation is steadily increasing due to two-income families with parents who are both working or single parents who are out doing the best they can to provide. Studies have concluded that "latchkey kids" struggle with loneliness, fear, insecurity, boredom, and more serious issues. I'm not judging other parents for the decisions they make because people do what they have to do to survive. But the decisions they make can be hard on children—even in their teenage years.

I live in a middle-class neighborhood, but I can drive up the road and see mansions. A few years ago, my family and I took a ride through some of the nearby neighborhoods just to look at the beautiful homes. When we came to one of the mansions, my son yelled out, "Hey, I know the kid that lives there. I go to school with him." Then I heard a sad story of how many of the kids who seemed to "have it all" were really struggling emotionally because no one was ever home. Some of them used drugs to numb the pain of feeling abandoned by their parents. What good is it to live in a big house full of beautiful things but be empty inside? I wished I could ask the parents if it was really worth it. Houses can be replaced, but if you lose your child, you may never get them back.

When my husband and I got married, he had to travel a lot for his job, and we didn't live near any family. So together we made a decision that I would give up my career and be a stay-at-home mom. We had bills to pay and sure could have used two incomes, but we felt that our children's security and well-being were more important than anything. We struggled in our small, two-bedroom apartment for a number of years, but Mom was home. When I look at my children today—now, they are officially adults—I see that they were well worth the investment and the sacrifices we made along the way. Even if there is no one there for you, I want you to know that you have not been forgotten!

WHEN PARENTS MESS UP

Speaking from experience, I can tell you that all parents make mistakes. We learn by trial and error as we go through the journey of raising children. It's only by the grace of God that any of us turn out decent because it's only when we allow God to shape our lives by His mighty hand that we can ever come to be who we are truly created to be.

Despite what your parents have done, or failed to do, don't spend your life blaming them for what has happened to you. Be willing to take responsibility for your own life and future. Many adults struggle through life and don't accomplish anything because of what their parents did or didn't do when they were kids. This is nothing more than making excuses and at some point, failing to take responsibility. Just know that wherever you are right now, God has allowed it for a reason. He sees you, and He will hear you if you cry out to Him for help.

WHEN ABRAHAM MESSED UP

Even Abraham, whom the Bible calls the father of faith, messed up things for his family, but God still took care of the situation. God had promised him and his wife, Sarah, a child, but after they grew old and nothing happened, they decided to take matters into their own hands. Abraham chose to have a child with one of Sarah's maids. Once the boy who resulted got to be a little older, the child God had promised Abraham and Sarah was born. So now we have one man with two children by two different women. Sounds complicated, doesn't it?

Just like in Bible times, it's not uncommon these days to see blended families or families where there are half-brothers and half-sisters in the same household. But all too often, these situations can lead to sibling rivalry because of the differences in parents, personality traits, and more—not to mention jealousy. When Abraham and Sarah had their son, Isaac, Abraham's other son—born to the maid Hagar—began to tease and taunt Isaac. Eventually, Sarah demanded that her husband kick the other woman and boy out of the house. The child was just being a child; it wasn't his fault how he came into the world, but he and his mom were kicked out of the house with only enough bread and water to last them a short time.

That was not the end of the story, though. Genesis 21 tells us:

> *God heard the boy crying and the angel of God called to Hagar from heaven, "Hagar, what's wrong? Do not be afraid! God has heard the boy crying as he lies there." —vv. 17-18 (NLT)*

Even when parents mess up, God still hears the prayers of the sons and daughters.

WHERE DO YOU TURN?

It's horrible when you feel like running and have nowhere to go. It's a horrible thing to have no peace in your life, not even at home or at school. What do you do? Whom do you lean on when you have no place to go? Abraham's son Ishmael cried out to God for help, and God heard. It wasn't his mother's cries that captured God's attention; it was the boy's.

You are a part of a unique generation, a technologically driven one that loves to engage in social media and listen to music with headphones. I believe the reason so many teens love noise is because there are so many voices bombarding them that they do whatever it takes to block them out. It may be to quiet the voices you don't want to hear or an attempt to deaden the pain in your heart that screams out moment by moment to remind you of what you would rather forget. But if you can find the courage to get alone in a "quiet place" where it's just you and God, you will be amazed by what will happen. There is peace and comfort in God's presence that you cannot find anywhere else in the world. It's not in the music you listen to. Neither is it found on television nor in movies. And it's not in other people.

> THERE IS PEACE AND COMFORT IN GOD'S PRESENCE THAT YOU CANNOT FIND ANYWHERE ELSE IN THE WORLD.

"Are you tired? Worn out? Burned out on religion?
Come to me. Get away with me and you'll recover
your life. I'll show you how to take a real rest. Walk
with me and work with me—watch how I do it. Learn
the unforced rhythms of grace. I won't lay anything
heavy or ill-fitting on you. Keep company with
me and you'll learn to live freely and lightly."
—Matthew 11:28-30 (MSG)

With peer pressure, homework assignments, extracurricular activities, or just keeping up with your friends, there are a lot of demands placed on your time. Maybe your parents are performance-driven, and you feel like you can never do enough to please them, so you work as hard as you can as long as you can, just trying to be your best. It's not surprising that so many teens are stressed out and overwhelmed by the pressures of life. Many even take extreme measures just to find ways to escape the pressure and simply cope with everyday life. For some, misusing prescription drugs or taking illegal substances, is their way of escape. For others, drinking or having sex is a normal part of their everyday life. And some teens are so full of the pain of rejection or abuse that they cut themselves to ease the greater pain they feel inside. But none of these things are the answer. These things will only leave you feeling worse in the end.

Maybe you haven't gone to such drastic measures, but you have found other ways of coping with your problems. No matter what you do to deal with your problems, it's just a temporary fix if you're not turning to God. Replacing God with other things will only lead you deeper into despair and take you further away from God's plan for your life. God has something better than what you are experiencing right now.

This is why God says, "Come!" He has provided a place of escape for you when you just can't take it anymore. He is your refuge, your hiding place, your place of safety and protection. God is always waiting for you to come to Him. He wants to hear what you have to say.

COME CLOSER!

You can depend on God when you can't count on anyone else, and He will always be there when you cry out to Him for help.

Where do you turn when life gets overwhelming? What is God speaking to you through this chapter?

_____

_____

_____

_____

_____

_____

_____

_____

_____

_____

_____

_____

_____

Prayer: "Lord, thank You for never leaving me or forsaking me. I will turn to You for help."

CHAPTER THREE

COME TO KNOW HIM

In every relationship, the more you hang out with someone the better you get to know them. We learn all about their personality, how they think, what makes them happy, and what they like and dislike. Getting to know God works the same way. The more you spend time alone with God the more you will get to know Him.

It's one thing to know of someone, but it's another to really know them personally. For example, if you were to stop and think of your favorite Hollywood star or singer, and someone were to ask you if you had ever heard of that person, you would probably say something like, "Yeah, I just love them! They are my favorite. . . ." Your answer would be based on what you know of them—secondhand information—not on what you know about them from firsthand experience. Wouldn't it be much better to be able to meet your favorite singer or actor and spend time with them, getting to know them personally?

Prayer gives you the opportunity to spend time with God, talk to Him, listen for His voice, and get to know Him personally.

> ## OFTENTIMES, WE GET OUR VIEW OF GOD FROM OUR EARTHLY FATHERS, FOR GOOD OR BAD.

How many times have you misjudged someone before you really got to know them and later realized they were nothing like you thought? It's the same with God. We all develop certain misconceptions about Him before we really take the time to know Him for ourselves. As you get to know God better, you will probably find that He is different than what you imagined. Oftentimes, we get our view of God from our earthly fathers, for good or bad.

When I was growing up, my father was a kind and loving man who wanted the best for me, so that's how I've always viewed God. But I have friends who never knew their dad, or they didn't have a good relationship with him, so they had a hard time seeing God as a loving, caring and compassionate Father who wants the best for them. Maybe you're the same—you have a hard time viewing God as a loving father. If so, that's okay. As soon as you start spending time with God, you will get to know His heart towards you, and you will see how good He is and how much He loves you.

Many people see God as a big, powerful God who sits on His throne, watching and waiting to strike them down or punish them for doing something wrong. Yes, He is big, and He is all-powerful, but He's not angry and full of rage towards His children. He is full of love! God is a loving Father, perfect in every way. He's not calling you to come and get your punishment; He's calling you to receive your blessings. Satan doesn't want you to receive what God has for you, so he does whatever he can to keep you from spending time with God. You have to be determined to not let anything or anyone stand in your way—not even yourself!

Prayer is all about coming to know God for yourself, not from what someone has told you about Him. Prayer is simply talking to God about life—telling Him what's on your heart, how you feel, and what you've been going through. Prayer is asking God for what you need and asking Him to help you. Nothing is off-limits. You speak directly to your heavenly Father, in Jesus's name, and after you have said what you want to, don't forget to give God a chance to speak to you because prayer is a two-way conversation. It's not just you talking to God, but it's also listening and allowing Him to speak to your heart. It's allowing Him to have a chance to reveal things to you that He wants you to know.

I don't know about you, but I don't like having conversations with people who don't give me a chance to say anything. I think it is rude and selfish; the conversation is all about them. One-sided conversation is no way to build a real relationship. In fact, a one-sided conversation really isn't a conversation at all. It's a monologue, not a dialogue.

KNOWING GOD'S VOICE

"My sheep know My voice, and I know
them, and they follow Me."
—John 10:27 (CEV)

One of the best things about prayer is hearing God speak to your heart. You may feel as though God never speaks to you, but maybe you just haven't taken time to really listen. Learning to hear and know the voice of the Lord is something that doesn't just happen. It's not until you begin to develop the discipline of spending time alone with God and being quiet in His presence that you can hear what He has to say.

> ## ONE OF THE BEST THINGS ABOUT PRAYER IS HEARING GOD SPEAK TO YOUR HEART.

The conversation of prayer is no different than any other conversation between two individuals. Someone talks while the other person listens; if two people talk at the same time, neither hears what the other has to say. When we first learn to pray, we have a tendency to do the majority of the talking because we have so much to say, so many needs and desires. But learning the art of listening is what makes prayer fun and exciting.

IS GOD SPEAKING TO ME?

The voice of the Lord is distinctively different from all others. It's just like recognizing a friend's voice when they call you on the phone, or your parents' voices when they call your name from another room in the house. If you talk to someone often enough, after a while you know their voice no matter what. Even if they try to disguise it you still recognize them.

There are many voices speaking into your life on a daily basis: your parents, family members, friends, teachers, coaches, and other leaders. Then there is the culture and the music you may listen to. All these voices are speaking into your life—not to mention the enemy, who will speak lies to you about yourself and try to lead you down the wrong path. This is why it's so important to know the Lord's voice above all other voices. This is accomplished by spending time with Him each day.

A STILL SMALL VOICE

"But the LORD was not in the wind. After the wind there was an earthquake, but the LORD was not in the earthquake. After the earthquake there was a fire, but the LORD was not in the fire. And after the fire came [a sound of gentle stillness] a still, small voice."
—1 Kings 19:11-12 (AMP)

God's voice is not loud and overbearing—you can miss it if you're not paying attention. If you always surround yourself with noise, like the television, loud music, and even other people's voices, it will be difficult to hear what God has to say. You must get alone with God in a quiet place.

I first began to hear God speak to my heart when I was a child, playing quietly by myself. His voice was as familiar as my mom's. There were times when I heard God calling my name, and I thought for sure it was my mother. I would call out to her to see if she had just called, but she would always tell me no. I didn't hear an audible voice, but it was so clear that it sounded like someone calling from a nearby place. The sound of God's voice is like a whisper in your ear.

When God was calling my name, I really didn't know it was Him. It wasn't until I became an adult and more spiritually mature that I realized that it was the Lord calling me to come to Him at a young age because He loved me and wanted to spend time with me.

SAMUEL LEARNS TO LISTEN

Samuel the Prophet was dedicated to the Lord even before he was born. His mother had been unable to have children until she cried out to God in prayer. She promised God that if He would bless her with a son, she would give him back. God heard and answered her prayers. Two years after her son was born, Hannah weaned him and took him to live in the temple with the priest.

One day when Samuel was lying down, he heard someone calling his name. He thought it was Eli the priest, so he ran to see what Eli wanted. Eli told Sam that he hadn't called and sent Sam back to his bedroom. This happened four times until Eli finally realized that it was the Lord that Sam had been hearing. He told the boy to go back to his room and when he heard the voice again, to respond by saying, "Speak, LORD, for your servant hears" (1 Samuel 3:9, ESV).

Samuel came to know the Lord's voice at an early age, and when he grew, he accomplished great things for God. If God spoke to Samuel when he was only a boy, do you think He can speak to you while you're young? I believe God has a specific purpose for your life, and it is never too early to discover just what He has created you to do. As you come to know the Lord through prayer and reading the Bible, God will begin to reveal His plan for your life.

HOW DOES GOD SPEAK?

"Be still, and know that I am *God."*
—Psalm 46:10a

God can speak to us through His written Word, the Bible. He can speak to us through people—especially those in one of the five-fold ministry offices such as apostles, prophets, evangelists, preachers, and teachers. You can be listening to a message on a podcast, and something is said that you know is just for you. God can also speak directly to your heart through the still small voice of the Holy Spirit who lives inside you as a born-again Christian. But in order to hear His voice, it's best to go to a quiet place to pray and ask God to speak to you. There is nothing wrong with enjoying music, watching television, playing video games, or spending time on social media sites, but if you really want to hear God speak to your heart, you have to position yourself to listen by turning off the noise in your life to spend time in prayer.

Being still and discovering what God is saying is a very important part of prayer. It's a necessary life skill that you will learn best through practice. Sometimes, God won't speak anything for long periods of time. Sometimes, He speaks more frequently. So be patient, and don't get discouraged if you don't hear God saying anything. God speaks to us when and how He wants to. Oftentimes I'll wake up in the morning with an awareness of God speaking something specific to my heart for that coming day. Sometimes He reveals things to me through dreams, or He makes a subtle impression on my heart. Sometimes I see things in my mind's eye, like an imagination. These are just some of the ways God may speak to you as you begin to develop a closer relationship with Him.

I've learned the hard way not to jump up in the morning and run full speed ahead into the day. Whenever I do, things always seem to go wrong! Now, when I open my eyes, before I put one foot on the floor I try to be still for a moment, listen, and direct my thoughts upward to God. I try to always remember to greet Him by saying good morning. I thank Him for waking me up and giving me the gift of another day.

It's something I have to be disciplined about. I usually charge my cell phone overnight and keep it next to my bed, so it's really tempting to grab it right away and start checking emails or see if anyone has texted me. Or I just might be silly enough to check to see what's on social media, as if I can't live without knowing what other people are doing or saying. The best thing, though, is to put God first and seek Him before doing anything else.

Life seems to be getting busier, and if we don't seek God at the beginning of the day, we may not get a chance to do so until much later. That's like putting God off until we have time for Him. God deserves to be first!

REAL TALK

Has there ever been a time when you needed to talk to someone about something going on in your life, and you felt like you had no one you could confide in? Have you ever done something wrong and you were afraid to tell anyone about it? Maybe there are times when you feel that no one understands you or cares about what's going on in your life.

> YOU CAN TELL YOUR HEAVENLY FATHER YOUR DEEPEST THOUGHTS, FEELINGS, AND SECRETS. YOU CAN TELL HIM ANYTHING. YOUR SECRETS ARE SAFE WITH HIM.

The good news is God knows and understands it all. Your heavenly Father is the One you should turn to no matter what. You can tell Him your deepest thoughts, feelings, and secrets. You can tell Him anything. Your secrets are safe with Him. God will not embarrass you. He won't talk to other people about you behind your back. He won't betray you, or lie to you. He won't reveal your secrets to anyone else. He is the most faithful and trustworthy friend you'll ever have.

When you talk to God, all He wants is for you to be honest with Him. He wants you to talk to Him from a sincere heart. It's like when your mom or dad ask you a question to which they already know the answer, just to see if you will be honest and tell the truth, even if it might get you into trouble. God already knows your thoughts, what you're up to when nobody's looking, and everything else. So you may as well tell Him what you really think and feel. Believe me, He can handle it! If I'm angry about something, God knows it, so I just tell Him, "Lord, I'm mad!" Then I continue the conversation.

Learning how to talk to God from your heart isn't hard. All you have to do is talk. It takes time to get to know someone well enough to trust them. Sometimes we trust other people more than we trust God. If there was ever someone to trust with your problems, it's God. He has the answer to every situation in your life. But He won't force His way in on you. You have to ask for His help. He will patiently wait until you're tired of life the way it is. The more you spend time with God, the more you will start to trust Him. After you clear your heart of the things you have been holding in, God can step in and help you. He will give you direction on how to handle the things you bring to Him. He may lead you into His Word by giving you a scripture that is an answer to your problem.

PRAYING GOD'S WORD

Once you have emptied out your heart before the Lord, you should pray God's Word back to Him. God's Words are His promises to you. Whatever He has said in His Word, He will do. So search through the Bible, and find scriptures that fit your situation. This is a process that takes time, but it is well worth it. The more you do this, the easier it will become and you will enjoy learning more about God. Praying the Word is like pleading your case in court. It is how you build your case with the Lord (Isaiah 43:26). Think of it like this: when your mom or dad has given you their word that they would do something, don't you hold them to it, and remind them of it until they make good on what they promised? God's Word is no different.

It is important to have a Bible concordance that you can use as a reference when you are looking for scriptures. Concordances help you to find any scripture that is in the Bible. Whenever you make special time for prayer, always make sure you have a Bible, a notebook or journal, and a pen to hand. I use journals because you can keep them for years, and always go back and read through them to see how God has answered past prayers. It's amazing to reflect back and remember the goodness of the Lord. It is a constant reminder of how much our Father loves us.

DOES HE HEAR MY PRAYERS?

"And we are confident that He hears us whenever we ask for anything that pleases him. And since we know he hears us when we make our request, we also know that He will give us what we ask for."
—1 John 5:14-15 (NLT)

God wants you to come to Him with confidence. He also wants to give you what you ask for. But whenever you do something that goes against God's Word, it will rob you of your confidence to pray. When you talk to God you have to be ready to turn away from sinful habits, and you have to come to Him with a pure heart that forgives others of what they have done to you. This will boost your confidence. What's even more important is to pray in agreement with what the Bible says. It's possible to go against God's Word or His will for your life. You have to know what the Bible says so that you can know how to pray prayers that align with God's Word.

DOES GOD ANSWER EVERY PRAYER?

God answers prayer in His own way and in His own timing. Sometimes He sends answers before we can barely finish praying. Sometimes God answers, "Yes, but not now," so the answer will come after a long season of waiting. Sometimes, His answer is no when we ask for something that is not His will for our lives.

> GOD ANSWERS PRAYER IN HIS OWN WAY AND IN HIS OWN TIMING. GOD NEVER ANSWERS US ACCORDING TO OUR TIMING AND OUR PLANS BECAUSE HE HAS HIS OWN PLANS AND AGENDA.

God never answers us according to our timing and our plans because He has His own plans and agenda. And His plan is always whatever is best for us. Now, God can't answer prayers that He doesn't hear. When you have a hard time forgiving others, you may spend time in prayer, but your prayers will go unheard. If you have sin in your heart, the Lord will not hear you (Psalm 66:18). When you pray out of a pure heart that is free from sin, God will hear and answer. I can still remember a simple prayer of mine as a child. I asked, "God, how will I know my husband when he comes? Will you show me who he is in a dream?" God had given me dreams at different times in my life to let me know that He was with me, and they would always bring me comfort. I knew He could show me my husband if I only asked. Having spoken to God about what was on my heart, I forgot about the prayer until many years later.

When I was about twenty-one years old, I had a very vivid dream that I was getting married. It was so real that when I woke up I felt as if it had really happened. In the dream I was at the altar of a church getting married to the man who is now my husband. When I had the dream, I had only just met him and we had never even been on a date. I told my mom about the dream and she didn't know what to make of it, but I held the dream in my heart until the day it became a reality.

God hears simple, childlike prayers from a sincere heart. There are no limits to what God can reveal to you in prayer. He didn't answer my prayer when I was a child, but at the appropriate time, He sent the answer.

COME CLOSER!

The more time you spend talking to God and listening, the better you will come to know Him and recognize when He is speaking.

Has God ever spoken to you? If so, what did He say? What has God been speaking to you through this chapter?

_____

_____

_____

_____

_____

_____

_____

_____

_____

_____

_____

Prayer: "Father, I want to know Your voice. Please help me to recognize when You're speaking to me."

CHAPTER FOUR

PRAYER 101

Prayer is not a religious requirement, something we must do to keep God from being angry with us. Prayer is not something to check off our *things-to-do list*. Prayer is not supposed to be a burden to us or something that we dread. Prayer is a privilege. It comes from a natural desire to spend time with God just because we love Him, and want to have a real relationship with Him. We pray because we're thankful for all that He has done for us. We pray because we need God, and we can't live without him. Prayer is our humble response to God's hands and heart extended toward us.

> **PRAYER IS OUR HUMBLE RESPONSE TO GOD'S HANDS AND HEART EXTENDED TOWARDS US.**

Jesus made a way for us to come to God boldly and confidently. Jesus came to earth to redeem us, justify us, sanctify us, and forgive our sins. Then He went back to heaven and sat down right next to God. Today, Jesus is praying for us. He prays that we will walk in love and learn to forgive one another the same way we have been forgiven of our wrongs. In John 19:30, as Jesus hung on the cross and drew His final breath, He uttered, "It is finished!" If He was willing to do all that He did for us, we should be willing to take the next step towards Him.

It takes humility to pray. When a person turns to God they are admitting that they need Him. But pride says, "I got this! I don't need anybody, not even God." The moment we talk or even think this way, the devil has us right where he wants us. However, the book of James says:

> God opposes the proud but favors the humble. So
> humble yourselves before God. Resist the devil, and
> he will flee from you. Come close to God, and God
> will come close to you. —James 4:6b-8a (NLT)

Thankfully, the Word doesn't just tell us to come near to God; Jesus actually taught us how to do it. He taught His disciples how to live everyday life. One of the most important skills He taught them was how to pray. He wanted them to know everything they needed to know in order to survive and be victorious over the devil.

The famous passage of scripture known as The Lord's Prayer is really the Lord teaching on how to pray. This is a model or pattern for prayer that you can use as a guide in your prayer time.

YOUR SECRET PLACE

*"When you pray, go into a room alone and close
the door. Pray to your Father in private. He knows
what is done in private and will reward you."*
—Matthew 6:6 (CEV)

The secret place is where God is. It is your safe place—somewhere you go to meet with God in private. You can share your secrets with Him, and He will share His secrets with you.

This secret place isn't a building or a literal location on earth; it is where we connect with God. He meets with us, and we meet with Him. The secret place is where to run to when you're overwhelmed by life, and you don't know what to do. It's the place to run to when you need help, peace, and comfort. The writer of Psalm 31 says, "You shall hide them in the secret place of Your presence, from the plots of man; You shall keep them secretly in a pavilion, from the strife of tongues" (v. 20, AMP). When you feel like escaping from the troubles of this world, the secret place is the place to be.

God leaves it up to us to pick our own private place to be alone with Him. It can be wherever you want—your bedroom, a closet, the garage, or the basement . . . anywhere that you can meet God in private.

For me, the secret place was upstairs in the attic of my childhood home. I would sneak off there whenever I felt overwhelmed or just wanted to talk to God. No one knew where I was, not even my parents. They didn't know that I was having private conversations with God. I was bullied as a child. I was bullied every day on the bus going to and from school. I was even bullied on the playground during recess. I never bothered anyone, so I couldn't figure out why I was picked on. I kept to myself and minded my own business, but that didn't matter. Looking back, I realize how my quiet and shy tendencies attracted the bullies' attention. It was as if I wore a sign on my forehead that said, "Hey, pick me. I'm an easy target."

One day, I was riding the bus home from school, and one of the bullies harassed me all the way to the bus stop. I felt the anger welling up within me; I'd had all I could take. When the bus finally stopped at the drop-off point, which was another school, I got off and grabbed the bully with both hands. With a power and strength unknown to my skinny frame, I lifted him high off the ground and threw him. The kids that had crowded around began to roar and laugh at him. He became so angry and embarrassed that he balled up his fist and punched me in the nose as hard as possible. I fell to the ground with my nose bleeding profusely. With the help of a friend, I went into the principal's office. To my amazement, the principal did nothing. The bully walked away as if nothing had happened. When I got home and told my mom what happened, she was furious. She wanted to drive to the boy's house a few blocks away and confront him and his parents, but I begged and pleaded for her not to. I thought it would only make matters worse.

I don't remember what I said to God in secret that day, but I knew He would do something about it. And from that day forward, I never had a problem with that bully again.

God cares about everything we go through, and His ears are always listening to our cries for help. It saddens me when I hear the reports of teenagers who have committed suicide because they were tired of being bullied. That is what happens when people don't know God or have a real relationship with Him. When people don't know how to cope, and they feel they have nowhere to turn, they take what they believe to be the only way out. But suicide is not the answer!

> **GOD CARES ABOUT EVERYTHING WE GO THROUGH, AND HIS EARS ARE ALWAYS LISTENING TO OUR CRIES FOR HELP.**

When I went into my bedroom to be alone with the Lord, I didn't realize I was following Jesus's teaching on prayer. He instructed us to go to a private place and pray to God in secret. He promised that the God who sees us in the secret place would reward us in the open (Matthew 6:6).

"For in the day of trouble He will hide me in His shelter; in the secret place of His tent will He hide me; He will set me high upon a rock."
—Psalm 27:5 (AMP)

No matter what kind of problems you may be facing, God sees and knows what you are going through. He has a way of escape for you, but you must come to Him for help. God can take care of a situation like no one else can. He is there for you when you have no one else to turn to. You can trust Him! Whenever life gets tough, cry out to God for help.

THE REWARDS

"Anyone who wants to come to Him must believe that God exists and that He rewards those who sincerely seek Him."
—Hebrews 11:6b (NLT)

When we spend time in prayer, God is pleased. It shows that we love Him and need Him and that we appreciate all He has done for us. The more we spend time with God, the more we are changed by His presence. And if that's not enough, God also rewards us with blessings and special favor. Favor is when good things happen to us even if we didn't do anything special to deserve it. If you had a rich friend who really loved you, they would probably do nice things for you every now and then, but God will be better to you than that. God has so many blessings in store for you as you get to know Him better.

Experiencing God's presence is a reward. Hearing God speak to your heart is a reward. Having peace of mind instead of confusion is a reward. Receiving God's love and comfort when you are hurting is a reward. Receiving answers to your prayers is a reward. Some of God's blessings are things that we sometimes take for granted, but we would never want to live without them. Here are just a few:

Comfort: "And I will ask the Father, and He will give you another Comforter (Counselor, Helper, Intercessor, Advocate,

Strengthener, and Standby), that He may remain with you forever." (John 14:16, AMP)

Guidance: "I will instruct you and teach you in the way you should go; I will guide you with My eye." (Psalm 32:8)

Help: "God is our refuge and strength, a very present help in trouble." (Psalm 46:1, ESV)

Hope: "For You are my hope, O Lord GOD; *You are* my trust from my youth. (Psalm 71:5)

Joy: "You will show me the path of life; in Your presence is fullness of joy." (Psalm 16:11a)

Love: "Behold what manner of love the Father has bestowed on us, that we should be called children of God!" (1 John 3:1a)

Peace: "Peace I leave with you, My peace I give to you; not as the world gives do I give to you. Let not your heart be troubled, neither let it be afraid." (John 14:27)

Protection: "He who dwells in the secret place of the Most High Shall abide under the shadow of the Almighty. . . . No evil shall befall you, nor shall any plague come near your dwelling, for He shall give His angels charge over you, to keep you in all your ways." (Psalm 91:1, 10-11)

Strength: "Be strong in the Lord [be empowered through your union with Him]; draw your strength from Him [that strength which His boundless might provides]." (Ephesians. 6:10, AMP)

Wisdom: "If any of you lacks wisdom, let him ask of God, who gives to all liberally and without reproach, and it will be given to him." (James 1:5)

Sometimes, life will get in the way and try to crowd out your time with God. But if you develop the discipline of spending time in prayer every day, you will be rewarded. The Bible tells us to pray without ceasing (1 Thessalonians 5:17). Pray every day, and pray often. God doesn't want you to pray because you have to; He wants you to do it because you want to. Pray because you need God. Pray for the purpose of getting to know God better. Pray because you are thankful for all He has done for you. Pray simply because you love God.

PRAYING LIKE JESUS

"Our Father in heaven, may Your name be kept holy. May Your Kingdom come soon. May Your will be done on earth, as it is in heaven. Give us today the food we need, And forgive us our sins, As we have forgiven those who sin against us. And don't let us yield to temptation, but rescue us from the evil one."
—Matthew 6:6-13 (NLT)

Pray to God the Father: *"Our Father in heaven, may Your name be kept holy" (v. 9).*

Talk directly to God your heavenly Father. As you acknowledge God, always speak to Him respectfully and worshipfully, giving honor and glory to His name. Praying to Jesus is like asking your brother for what you want instead of going directly to your parents. When Jesus was on the earth, He prayed to God the Father, not to Himself. Jesus is God's Son, and we are God's children. Once we have accepted Jesus as our personal Lord and Savior, we can pray to God in the name of Jesus, and God will hear our prayers. And always start your prayers with praise and thanksgiving; remembering what God has done for you makes it easy to start the conversation of prayer.

Pray for God's will: *"May Your Kingdom come soon. May Your will be done on earth, as it is in Heaven" (v. 10).*

There is nothing wrong with asking God for what you want. He wants to give you the desires of your heart. But also remember to pray for God's will to be done in every situation because His will is higher than your own personal will. When you pray this way, you are giving up what you want and choosing what God wants for you instead. You are praying for God's best for your life.

Pray for your daily needs: *"Give us today the food we need" (v. 11).*

Take things one day at a time. Pray and ask for what you need for today, not tomorrow. Maybe you are going to take an important test at school, so you can ask God to help you to do well. The Lord doesn't want you to be worried or overwhelmed about tomorrow or the next day but to deal with your life one day at a time.

Pray to forgive others and to be forgiven: *"Forgive us our sins as we forgive those who sin against us" (v. 12).*

Pray and ask for forgiveness for the things you do wrong each day. You also must be sure to forgive others, releasing them from the wrong things they do to you, whether or not they hurt you intentionally. If you don't forgive others, the Lord will not forgive you. How can you hold a grudge against someone who has treated you wrong, and then turn around and go to God in prayer and ask Him to forgive you for the things you do wrong? It doesn't match up, does it?

Pray against temptation and evil: *"Keep us from being tempted and protect us from evil" (v. 13).*

The temptation to do wrong may surround you, but you don't have to fall into the trap of being tempted. If you ask God to deliver you from being tempted and help you to be strong, He will. Ask the Lord to keep you in His care, and protect you from doing wrong and from wrong things happening to you. If your heart is to do what is right, God will help you. In 1 Chronicles 4, we read of a mother who named her son Jabez because she was in great pain when she gave birth to him. But Jabez didn't want to be associated with causing others pain, so he prayed and asked God to bless him and enlarge his territory. He asked God to be with him and keep him from evil, and not allow him to cause others pain, and God gave Jabez what he asked for (v. 10).

GETTING STARTED

Coming to God is not a one-time event. You come daily! Now that you know the flow of prayer, your time spent with God will be much easier. If you follow Jesus's teaching on prayer and talk to God from your heart, you really can't go wrong. Here are some helpful steps:

- ♦ Pick a time of day that is the best time for you to pray. Setting aside a specific time for prayer will help you to establish a routine. This is very beneficial, and it has helped me to be more diligent and consistent in prayer. I've found mornings are best for me because otherwise it's easy to let all the things that need to be done to crowd out time with God, but another time might work better for you. Just be sure to keep that appointment!

♦ Determine where you want to pray. Remember, it's your choice. You pick the place, and God will meet you there.

♦ Keep your Bible, a journal or notebook, and a pen with you when you pray. You can write down whatever God speaks to your heart. You can read the Word and find scriptures that deal with whatever you're going through. When you write down your prayers and whatever God speaks to your heart, you can look back and see what God has done for you.

> **IF YOU FOLLOW JESUS'S TEACHING ON PRAYER AND TALK TO GOD FROM YOUR HEART, YOU REALLY CAN'T GO WRONG.**

COME CLOSER!

Jesus gave us a guideline for prayer.

Which portion of the Lord's teaching on prayer stands out to you the most and why? Which of the rewards of prayer do you need in your life the most? What is God speaking to you through this chapter?

_____

_____

_____

_____

_____

_____

_____

_____

_____

_____

_____

_____

Prayer: "Heavenly Father, help me to pray the way Jesus taught in the Word."

CHAPTER FIVE

LET IT GO!

> *"If you forgive others for the wrongs they do to you,*
> *your Father in heaven will forgive you. But if you don't*
> *forgive others, your Father will not forgive your sins."*
> —Matthew 6:14-15 (CEV)

F orgiveness is a very important part of prayer. When the disciples approached Jesus asking Him to teach them how to pray, one of the things He told them was to ask God to forgive their debts as they forgave their debtors. If we forgive men their trespasses (the things they do against us), our heavenly Father will also forgive us—but if we do not forgive men their trespasses, neither will our Father forgive our trespasses (Matthew 6:12, 14-15). How can we ask God to do something for us that we won't do for others? We need to be forgiven of the things we do wrong, so we need to forgive others.

When we do what is right in the sight of God, He will take care of the rest. It's not our job to pay people back for the wrong things they do to us. God has a way of causing people to reap what they sow, and He does a much better job than we could ever do. It's simply the law of sowing and reaping.

Do you have issues with the way someone has treated you? Talk to God about it. He will take care of the situation for you. If you will be patient and wait on God, you won't be disappointed with the results. You will have peace of mind. You'll feel a release about the situation, which means it will no longer torment your mind. Whatever we turn over to Him, we are freed from, and it can't weigh us down any more.

Forgiving someone is not determined by the way you feel. It is a choice.

> TO FORGIVE IS A SUPERNATURAL WORK OF THE HOLY SPIRIT. IT IS NOT BASED ON HOW WE FEEL ABOUT OTHERS, OR EVEN OURSELVES, IT IS AN ACT OF OBEDIENCE.

If you choose to forgive, God can give you the grace to do it if you ask. We can't love and forgive people who hurt us without the supernatural power of God. Jesus said the following:

"It is impossible that no offenses should come, but woe to him through whom they do come! It is better for him if a millstone were hung around his neck, and he were thrown into sea, than that he should offend one of these little ones." —Luke 17:1-2

God sees and knows what has happened in your life. He wants you to come to Him with your pain and disappointment. He will show you any unforgiveness in your heart and then you can give it to Him. Unforgiveness is one of the chief reasons why prayers go unanswered. There was a man who asked Jesus how many times he had to forgive his brother for his wrongdoing. Jesus answered:

> *"Take heed to yourselves, If your brother sins against you, rebuke him; and if he repents, forgive him. And if he sins against you seven times a day, and seven times in a day returns to you, saying 'I repent,' you shall forgive him."* —Luke 17:3-4

If you want to keep things right between you and God, you have to be willing to forgive. When you hold on to the wrong things people do to you, that means you are carrying an offense or holding a grudge, and God can't move on your behalf. If you want to be forgiven, you must forgive. And if Jesus could forgive mankind and wipe the slate of sin clean, how can we not forgive one another?

LEARNING FROM OTHERS

The story of Joseph is one I can truly relate to. Even after his brothers plotted against him and sold him to slavery—going as far as to deceive their father into believing that he was dead—he didn't hold it against them. When later God raised Joseph up into a position of great power and authority, when he had a chance to let his brothers have it, instead he forgave them.

Look at what he said to them when they were reunited after many years, in Genesis 45:

*"Please come near to me. ... I am Joseph your brother,
whom you sold into Egypt. But now, do not therefore be grieved or angry with yourselves because
you sold me here; for God sent me before you to preserve life. And God sent me before you to preserve
a posterity for you in the earth, and to save your
lives by a great deliverance. So now it was not you
who sent me here, but God; And He has made me
a father to Pharaoh, and lord of all his house, and
a ruler throughout all the land of Egypt."* —vv. 4-8

What a great attitude! Joseph trusted God and kept his heart
right, knowing that God would take care of him and make
everything right. Whether it is your family, or even your parents, who have mistreated you, if you keep your heart right
with God by not holding on to unforgiveness, He will lift you
up and make your life significant. The book of Psalms is full
of prayers by David. I love the Psalms because they express
the heart of a man who knew how to cry out to God from the
depths of his pain. He suffered a lot in his lifetime, but he never
failed to rely on God for help.

When David was a young boy, he struggled with family
issues similar to those of Joseph. First Samuel 17 tells how he
was out in the field, tending to the sheep, when Samuel the
prophet came to the house searching for Israel's next king. One
day, David's father, Jesse, sent him out to check on his brothers
who were in the army fighting against the Philistines. As soon
as he showed up, the brothers accused him of being prideful
and told him to go back home and tend to his few sheep. The

brothers treated David as if he were insignificant, but God had big plans for him! Here is one of David's prayers, from Psalm 27:

> *"You've always been right there for me; don't turn your back on me now. Don't throw me out, don't abandon me; you've always kept the door open. My father and mother walked out and left me, but God took me in."* —v. 10 (MSG)

YOU CAN DO IT!

If we hold a grudge against those who have mistreated us or abused us, then the Lord won't be able to help. Unforgiveness clogs up the flow of prayer in our life. When you try to pray about something, it's as if God doesn't even hear you.

When we forgive others for doing us wrong, it keeps the door open. We are free to go to God with our prayers and complaints so we can plead our cause before Him. If we lived in a perfect world, full of perfect people, we would all treat each other with dignity and respect. But that is not the world we live in.

Unfortunately, when people hurt other people, it's often because they are hurting themselves. When people do bad things to other people, many times it's linked to something that happened to them during childhood, or some life-changing event that left them traumatized. Most times people don't hurt people just because they are evil and want to cause pain, but it is an overflow of what's taking place inside their heart and mind. There is always a reason.

If you have been a victim of some form of abuse—whether physical, sexual, verbal, or emotional—God wants to heal you of your pain. You may have struggled with why God allowed these things to happen to you, and you may never quite understand until you see Him face to face. But God wants you to trust Him in spite of it all. And He wants to heal you and set you on a new path.

> ## FORGIVENESS IS AN IMPORTANT PART OF THE HEALING PROCESS.

Forgiveness is an important part of the healing process. It doesn't necessarily mean that the person who hurt you will come and acknowledge what they did. Many times, we have to forgive in spite of never hearing the words, "I'm sorry." Forgiving others is not an easy process, but it can be done.

It is as simple as making a decision that you don't want to be bound by what has happened to you. If you don't want to be defined by what took place in the past, but instead move forward into the good life God has planned for you, all you need to do is go to Him for help. He will give you the grace you need to overcome. He will help you do what you are not able to do on your own.

When Jesus was hanging on the cross, He gave His life for us—even for those who actually drove the nails into His hands and feet, who stuck the crown of thorns on His head, who pierced Him. And He said, "Father forgive them, for they don't know what they are doing" (Luke 23:34, NLT). God gave Him strength to forgive. To forgive is a supernatural work. It is not based on how we feel about others—or even ourselves. It's an act of obedience.

BUT WHAT IF I REALLY MESS UP?

"For You, Lord, are good, and ready to forgive, And abundant in mercy to all those who call upon You."
—Psalm 86:5

Messing up is what we do! None of us are perfect, even when we try to be. Living the Christian life is not a matter of perfection but of growth. We are all being transformed into the image of Christ. And God will work on us until Jesus returns to get us. We also have an enemy who would love more than anything to deceive us into believing that when we mess up, it's over for us, and there is no chance of having our fellowship and relationship with God restored. But nothing could be further from the truth. If we believe that lie, we will never know the assurance of our salvation, and we will never have the confidence necessary to approach God in prayer.

Whether you realize it or not, there are unseen forces that are always trying to keep us from God. If the devil could have his way, he would keep us from ever spending time with God. Why does he care about us spending time with God? Because it means everything to him. He doesn't want us to get close to God or to know God's love for us because the moment we do it will begin to transform our lives forever.

If we could really grasp this, Satan would no longer be able to trick us and deceive us because we would have an awareness of who we are in Christ and we would begin to know the power and authority we have over the power of darkness. When we do sin, we have an advocate with the Father—Jesus. He waits for us to come to Him with a repentant heart, one that is truly sorry for sins we've committed against God.

Repentance is nothing more than taking ownership of our wrongdoing. When we go before God in prayer He wants us to come clean about our mistakes, whether they are our actions, our words, or our thoughts. God already knows about them, but if we don't ask for forgiveness, how can we be forgiven? When we repent, we need to turn away from those things and not do them anymore. That's true repentance. When this is accomplished, we are no longer distant from God. We can freely go before Him, without feeling guilty and condemned. We no longer need to feel like God is angry with us. That is why Galatians 5:11 instructs Christians not to be enslaved again with the yoke of bondage, but to be free. Sin is bondage, and it's just like being caught in a net and trapped until we are set free.

DO I HAVE TO PAY FOR WHAT I DID WRONG?

When we were talking about sin and forgiveness, someone once asked me whether a girl who had sex, and then asked God to forgive her, would she still have to suffer the consequences.

I responded by saying yes, the girl would be forgiven and put back into right fellowship with God—but she may still have to face the consequences of pregnancy or perhaps some disease. This is an extreme example because not all girls get pregnant if they have sex, but the point is that could very well be the consequence of that action. The truth of the matter is all sin has a price tag attached to it, and sometimes the price is higher than what we're willing to pay.

We really can't play around with the devil because he never, ever plays fair. First, he leads us into sin through subtle temptation and the power of suggestion. Then, once he has lured us in and we do what he suggests, he beats us up over it! He talks about us to God saying, "Look! Look what they just did. They don't deserve to be blessed; they don't deserve to go to heaven." How low down and conniving is that? All he wants to do is go before God and accuse us of things because he's jealous. He messed up, and there is no way he can fix it.

But if Satan can get you to live under the weight of guilt and condemnation, he has won. You must learn from your mistakes, get up from where you have fallen, brush yourself off, and go to your heavenly Father. Humbly repent, and try again. God will give you the grace to do better. God will give you a fresh start and a new beginning. He will wash the slate clean and cast your sins into the sea of forgetfulness, never to be remembered again. Now, if God can forgive you, then you should be able to forgive yourself. When we refuse to forgive ourselves, we actually lift ourselves up higher than God, which is nothing more than pride. If you have messed up, forgive yourself, and receive God's forgiveness!

> **IF YOU HAVE MESSED UP, FORGIVE YOURSELF, AND RECEIVE GOD'S FORGIVENESS!**

PRAYER OF REPENTANCE:

"Heavenly Father, I humble myself before you, and I confess my sins of _____. I turn away from it now, and I ask you to give me a clean heart and renew a right spirit within me. Help me to never turn back from this day forward. According to 1 John 1:9, Your Word says that if we confess our sins, You are faithful and just to forgive us our sins and to cleanse us from all unrighteousness. I want to be righteous in Your sight so that I can be with You forever. I love You, and I receive Your gift of forgiveness. Please help me to walk upright before You. In Jesus's name, Amen!"

"Anyone who belongs to Christ is a new person.
The past is forgotten, and everything is new."
—2 Corinthians 5:17 (CEV)

Now that you have set things right with God, you can go to Him with boldness and confidence. You don't have to be afraid or ashamed. You are not rejected. You are loved and accepted by God, and He is waiting for you to *come*. Make today the day you embark on a fresh new love relationship with God that will last throughout eternity.

COME CLOSER!

If you forgive others for the wrongs they have done to you, God will forgive you for your wrongs.

Has someone hurt you or left you disappointed so that you can't seem to forget about what happened? Write their name(s) below. What is God speaking to you through this chapter?

_____

_____

_____

_____

_____

_____

_____

_____

_____

_____

Prayer: "Father God, these people have hurt me. I ask You to forgive them for what they have done to me, and I ask You to help me to forgive them and release the situation to You. Please give me the courage and strength to move forward. I ask You to help me forget what has happened, and heal me of the pain."

CHAPTER SIX

LOOKING FOR LOVE?

"Pay close attention! Come to Me and live. I will promise you the eternal love and loyalty that I promised David."
—Isaiah 55:3 (CEV)

Nobody cares.
Nobody has time for me.
I wish I had someone who really loved me.
Nobody wants me.
Maybe I'm ugly.
I'm too skinny.
Maybe I should just kill myself and get it all over with.

These thoughts once bombarded my mind; have you ever felt like this?

As a teenager, I was tormented by fear and feelings of loneliness and despair. I felt as though nobody really cared about me. Things got so bad at one point that I considered cutting myself. I got a knife from the drawer and put it to my wrist but didn't go through with it. Feelings of despair were leading me to end it all until God gently spoke and told me to put the knife away. God was there again when I needed Him. Most people would think that being the youngest in my family put me in the perfect position to be spoiled and get everything I wanted. But the opposite was true. It seemed to me as though everyone was busy with their own lives, doing their own thing, and had no time for me. I knew in my heart that my parents loved me, but they had issues of their own to deal with, so they never really understood how much I was struggling.

Oftentimes, when you feel like something is wrong with you, it's just the enemy coming against you to stop God's plan for your life. Satan is a master at mind games. He puts thoughts in our minds to try and convince us that his lies are true. Then he tries to make us believe those thoughts are ours. Being bombarded with thoughts of failure, loneliness or depression, and the temptation to give up are more common than you may think.

One of the best ways to combat Satan's lies is to expose him. When a person is struggling and feels like giving up, most times the people around them never really know the depths of their pain. This is because we don't tell anyone what we're going through. But if you were to go around and ask your friends if they have ever felt the way you may be feeling, you would be surprised by how many of them have had the same struggles.

It is important to know that what you're dealing with are classic signs of spiritual warfare—which lets you know that

God has a special purpose for your life! Think about it: why would the devil be trying to bring you down if you were a nobody or *if your life had no value*?

CREATED FOR LOVE

At some point in our lives, we've all experienced feelings of loneliness or rejection and the desire to be loved. No matter how much we look to people for the quantity and quality of love that would satisfy us, we seem to always fall short because no earthly or human love can compare to God's love. As a teenager, I was tall, thin, and average-looking. I didn't have the popularity that others did, so I was lost in the crowd. I would see other people with their boyfriends or girlfriends, and it made me want to be with someone too. I don't know what it is about human nature that equates being accepted by others with being loved. But acceptance is usually conditional, while real love is unconditional. I felt so lonely, and I wanted someone to think I was pretty. Really, I was looking for love.

Teenage years can be hard, especially when it comes to love. There are times when you can give your heart to someone, supposedly "falling in love," and have no intentions of marrying them, or even seeing them beyond high school. Not a smart thing to do! Why give away what is so valuable when it should actually be protected? Love is precious and something that shouldn't be awakened until the proper time, when you can really do something about it. Why fall in love when you're a teenager who still needs to discover your purpose in life? Why fall in love before you are really ready to get married?

Most times, when teenagers fall in love in high school the two people aren't heading in the same direction. Both people may choose to go to different colleges. Or one is planning to go to college and the other one doesn't want to go to college, or they don't have a clue about what they want to do. By the time people fall in love, they should be ready to make a commitment to spend the rest of their lives with the person they've given their heart to.

I'm not here to burst your bubble or kill your dreams of one day finding someone special, but I want to encourage you to think higher. In all reality, the teenage years are a time to discover who you are and who God is so that you can learn what real love is all about. When you have learned to receive God's love, love yourself, and love others—especially those who are not easy to love—then you know something about love.

> WHEN YOU HAVE LEARNED TO RECEIVE GOD'S LOVE, LOVE YOURSELF, AND LOVE OTHERS—ESPECIALLY THOSE WHO ARE NOT EASY TO LOVE—THEN YOU KNOW SOMETHING ABOUT LOVE.

Unfortunately, when we're young, what we think is real love is only infatuation or lust, and when we give in to them they can take us down a path to emotional turmoil, confusion, heartbreak, depression, and more. God wants you to experience real love. When you do, you will never be the same. God's love transforms us into beautiful, loving people who release a fragrance that is desirable to others. People are then drawn to us because they are drawn to the love of God in us.

A LESSON ON LOVE

When I entered high school, I was sold out to God. I loved Him, and I knew He loved me. But because I didn't have a boyfriend, I thought I was unattractive and unwanted. I felt rejected. The devil has a way of making sure he maximizes opportunities such as low self-esteem, rejection, and loneliness to accommodate us. So while I didn't go out and look for someone to love me, the devil sent someone into my life.

One day, as I was sitting in one of my classes, a friend told me to look out the door. There was a guy who supposedly liked me and wanted my phone number. I was gullible, excited that someone was interested in me. I wanted someone to spend time with and walk the halls with, so I took the bait. It wasn't long before we started going out. Sad to say, I spent the next few years with a guy that I didn't even marry.

That time was somewhat fun, but it was more filled with disappointment, depression, loneliness, and confusion. Does this sound familiar to you? What a waste of time and energy! Although he was a nice guy, we were so different from each other. I went to church; he didn't. I wanted to go to college; he didn't. I had dreams of doing something special with my life; he didn't know what he wanted. At one point he told me he wanted to marry me, but I knew we had no future together. Eventually, we broke up.

COME FOR LOVE

First Corinthians chapter 13 gives us a wonderful description of what love is and what it is not. Since God is love, we can get a good view of His nature from this well-known passage:

> Love is patient and kind.
> Love is not jealous or boastful or proud or rude.
> It does not demand its own way.
> It is not irritable, and it keeps no record of being wronged.
> It does not rejoice about injustice but rejoices whenever the truth wins out.
> Love never gives up, never loses faith, is always hopeful, and endures through every circumstance.
> —vv. 4-7 (NLT)

When you begin to spend time with God, you will begin to experience His love. You will see how patient He is with you when you make mistakes, and you will see how kind He is to you. The more you experience His love, the more loving you will be towards others. You will become more patient and kind. You won't be full of pride. You won't go around bragging about yourself. You won't be irritable, or have a hard time forgiving people when they treat you wrong.

It takes time to learn to receive the love of God, and it really takes time to learn how to love people—especially if they have done you wrong. Give yourself time to be loved by God before you go looking for love from people.

The Song of Solomon is a fascinating book. Its primary theme is love. Bible scholars and theologians tell us that there are three basic interpretations of the book. The first is that it is about a love relationship between a man and woman (Solomon and the Shulamite) as they head into marriage. The second interpretation is that it is a reflection of God's love relationship with Israel, His chosen people. The third interpretation is that it illustrates Jesus's love relationship with the church. Read the Song of Solomon for yourself; it is only eight chapters long. Before you begin, ask God to reveal its meaning and help you understand it. When you look at how beautiful the love relationship displayed in this book is, it will make you want to experience true love, which is God Himself.

> *"I charge you, O daughters of Jerusalem, By the gazelles or by the does of the field, Do not stir up nor awaken love Until it pleases."*
> —Song of Solomon 3:5

God doesn't want you to seek for love before you can handle it. He doesn't want you to give your heart to anyone other than Him because He doesn't want your heart to be broken. If you give your heart to someone who is incapable of loving to the degree that you need and desire to be loved, they will inevitably hurt you or disappoint you. Three times Song of Solomon charges us not to awaken feelings of love before the right time. Unless we are awakening our love for God and His love for us, then love is premature and it will only lead to brokenness.

GUARD YOUR HEART

If you want to avoid falling into the trap of trying to experience love before you are ready, then there are a few things you must do to protect yourself. You have to guard two main entry points—your eyes and ears. That's because you can stir up romantic feelings or feelings of lust through what you see and hear. Here are five ways to guard your heart from counterfeit love:

♦ Be watchful of music with lyrics talking about love and sex.

♦ Don't watch movies that are centered around sex, relationships, and promiscuity.

♦ Don't focus on what others are doing around you. The more you see other people hugged-up and kissing and being together, the more you will want to experience it. What glistens is not always gold! You have no idea what heartache awaits those involved in these relationships.

♦ Watch out for people who come into your life talking a good talk, telling you how good you look or how sexy you are. Even if you are handsome or gorgeous, this is only designed as a trap to distract you from your purpose and destiny.

♦ Focus on your purpose and what God has for you until He brings you the person He has for you.

> FOCUS ON YOUR PURPOSE AND WHAT GOD HAS FOR YOU UNTIL HE BRINGS YOU THE PERSON HE HAS FOR YOU.

LOVE AND SEX ARE NOT THE SAME

Sex is one of the wonderful ways we get to express love in marriage, but it is not love. The world has taken something God created specifically for a married couple's pleasure and to reproduce and perverted it. Sex has been cheapened to the point where it is not valued as precious or special.

Oftentimes, when a girl is looking for love, a guy may be looking for sex. Girls tend to want true love and even dream of the day they will get married and become moms, while guys typically want to enjoy the expression of love without true love or commitment.

This is not a fair exchange by any means. So it is up to you to know your value and worth. Don't get love and sex confused. Don't give your body and heart to someone other than your spouse on your wedding day. It is a gift that is way too valuable to abuse.

In essence, I'm advising you to beware of "falling in love" or becoming sexually active when you're young. If you haven't fallen in love with God first, why would He bring that special someone into your life for you to "fall in love" with before the right time? The answer is, He wouldn't. God knows when and how to bring the person He has for you into your life, at just the right time. He can cause two people who are just right for each other to cross paths at the right time in their lives. If you wait on God's timing for love, He will reward you. Fall in love with God and learn to love yourself so that you can appropriately love someone else.

The choices you make today will affect your life tomorrow, and the next day, and the day after that. One day you will be married and your children will ask you if you waited until you were married before you had sex. They will want to know all the details of how you fell in love. Believe it or not, your decisions and choices will play a part in your children's decisions and choices. Live a life of true love in God and save yourself for marriage so that you can speak without guilt and shame when you speak to your children.

COME CLOSER!

God is love, and in Him is found true unconditional love.

Where have you been looking for love and acceptance? What is God speaking to your heart through this chapter?

_____

_____

_____

_____

_____

_____

_____

_____

_____

_____

_____

_____

_____

Prayer: "Father God, reveal Your love to me, and help me to put You first in my life and make You my first love."

CHAPTER SEVEN

WHY AM I HERE?

One of the greatest questions we face in life is, why am I here? The question can lurk deep within our hearts until feelings of discontentment send us on a quest to find the answer. Even many adults, if they are honest, are still struggling to come to an awareness of their purpose, so why is it that teenagers are expected to know what they want to do with the rest of their lives when they are still young? After a total of thirteen short years of school, at eighteen, we are thrust into adult life, having to figure everything out and make some sense of it all. If we're really fortunate, our parents may see that we are leaning towards a particular gift or talent and point us in that direction. But oftentimes, even loving, well-meaning parents can't offer us very much guidance or assistance in terms of our destiny.

I discovered God's purpose for my life in the secret place. I had grown weary of my day-to-day activities, and I felt deep inside that there had to be more to life. After diligent prayer, I finally discovered my purpose. Even from child-hood, God placed within me a love for writing and a love for people. English was always my best subject in school, and my compassionate heart and gift of encouragement seemed to draw people to me. They would open up and share their struggles. In essence, I was created to encourage others and spread the good news of the gospel through books and teaching. God often takes those things that seem to come so easy and natural for us, and He uses them to bless others and bring glory to Himself. These natural tendencies are really gifts from God.

> GOD CREATED YOU FOR A SPECIFIC PURPOSE, BUT YOU HAVE TO SPEND TIME WITH HIM TO FIND OUT WHAT IT IS.

Do you know your purpose?

Can you identify the gifts, talents, and abilities God has given you?

If money were no object, what would you do with your life to make a difference in the world?

God created you for a specific purpose, but you have to spend time with Him to find out what it is. As you seek the Lord, He will begin to reveal His plan for your life. He will speak to your heart about the assignment He has for you.

It is a normal part of the process to go through a season of refinement. It qualifies you and prepares you for your destiny. It's in these times that you grow spiritually strong to do what God has created you to do. God wants to see just how determined you are about your purpose. God never intended for your life here on earth to be boring and mundane. He wants you to fulfill a specific purpose, live in your dreams, and arrive at your destiny. He wants you to be happy and fulfilled.

The late Dr. Myles Munroe, a pastor and best-selling author from Nassau, Bahamas, and one of the greatest teachers on the subject of purpose once said the following:

> *The cemetery is one of the richest places on earth because books, businesses, or the cure for a disease are all buried there because so many have died without fulfilling their purpose.*[2]

Some years ago, as I was listening to Dr. Monroe teach on purpose, he made a statement that was so simple and yet profound that I have never forgotten it. He said, "If you want to know the purpose of a thing you must look in the mind of the maker." Only God knows why He created each of us, and the sooner we seek Him concerning our purpose, the better. You are never too young to ask God what He has created you to do in life. Knowing your purpose can save you a lot of time, energy, trouble, and even money.

How often do we see college students suddenly switch degrees midstream? And what about those who go to school for one thing, and when they enter the real world and begin to work in the field of their choice, they discover that they hate their job? It's not unusual to see adults go back to school later in life so that they can do something altogether different from what they went for the first time around. Dr. Monroe also said,

---

2 Myles Monroe, Understanding Your Potential (Shippensburg, PA: Destiny Image Publishers, Inc., 1991) 15.

"Where purpose is not known, abuse is inevitable."[3] It's like trying to use a hammer to cut down a tree. The hammer was created for the purpose of hammering, not sawing. So whatever you are created to do, it is a misuse of your purpose to do anything else. And besides that, who wants to roam around aimlessly through life not knowing their purpose or having a sense of direction? Joy and fulfillment come when we live according to purpose.

DISCOVERING YOUR PURPOSE

> "Then the Word of the Lord came to me [Jeremiah] saying: 'Before I formed you in the womb I knew you; Before you were born I sanctified you; I ordained you a prophet to the nations.' Then I said, 'Ah, Lord God! Behold, I cannot speak, for I am a youth.' But the Lord said to me: 'Do not say, "I am a youth," For you shall go to all to whom I send you, and whatever I command you, you shall speak. Do not be afraid of their faces, for I am with you to deliver you,' says the Lord."
> —Jeremiah 1:4-8

From this passage, we can clearly see that Jeremiah had a relationship with God. He knew Him well enough to have a conversation about his purpose. There was a dialogue going on between the two of them. After being told what his life's purpose was, Jeremiah thought surely he was too young for the assignment, but God said otherwise. God told Jeremiah

---

3 Myles Munroe, *Understanding the Purpose & Power of Woman* (New Kensington, PA: Whitaker House, 2001) 31.

not to be concerned about his age, but to just do what he was commanded to do, and the Lord promised to be with him.

What is so wonderful about this is that Jeremiah knew how to pray at a young age. He didn't wait until he was a grown-up to start to have a relationship with the Lord. Because of this, God was able to reveal His divine plan and purpose for Jeremiah while he was young. Wouldn't you like to find out what your purpose is while you are young, rather than wasting a lot of time doing things that really don't mean anything in terms of your future? Payton and Eli Manning, Venus and Serena Williams, and Tiger Woods learned what their gifts and talents were early in life. They trained and practiced until they became great. Wouldn't you like to save time and energy and go in the direction of what God created you to do?

"I cry out to God Most High, to God who
will fulfill His purpose for me."
—Psalm 57:2 (NLT)

God not only gives us a purpose, but He also gives us all the gifts, and abilities we need to fulfill it.

Throughout our lives there are little clues that reveal our purpose, but sometimes we just don't pay attention because these are things that come easily or naturally to us. And they are always things we enjoy doing.

God would never have us spend a lifetime doing something we hate. He is not a cruel Father. He wants us to be happy and enjoy our lives.

We can spend time trying to figure out what we're supposed to do with our lives, or we can spend time with God and ask Him to reveal His plan and purpose for us.

> WE CAN SPEND TIME TRYING TO FIGURE OUT WHAT WE'RE SUPPOSED TO DO WITH OUR LIVES, OR WE CAN SPEND TIME WITH GOD AND ASK HIM TO REVEAL HIS PLAN AND PURPOSE FOR US.

We should never allow someone else to decide what we're going to do with our lives, nor should we depend on someone else to take charge. No one should care about your purpose more than you, and it's your responsibility to be determined to find out why you are here.

HOW I DISCOVERED MY PURPOSE

Towards the end of my high school years, I was forced to take a serious look at what I wanted to do with my life. I had enjoyed school for the most part, until I entered into the tenth grade. I don't know if the work was too hard for me, if I just wasn't applying myself, or a little of both. Whatever the reason, for the last two years I was there I hated school, and I couldn't wait to get out. The last thing I wanted was more schoolwork. So I started thinking about what I could do with my life that would actually be fun. I was an average student, so I knew I wasn't going to get a scholarship or be accepted into some prestigious institution of higher learning. But whatever I was planning to do was going to take money—something my family didn't have.

I was the youngest of six children, so by the time my parents had paid for my oldest sister's wedding and put three of my siblings through college, there was nothing left for me. I had to figure something out and make a way for myself. I knew I couldn't just sit around the house and do nothing. Deep within my heart, I knew I was created to do something of value with my life.

A couple of friends persuaded me to enter a scholarship cotillion. I was hoping to win the grand prize of a thousand-dollar scholarship; it could help give me some kind of start. Unfortunately I wasn't the winner, though I did get honorable mention, along with a trophy. More importantly I came away feeling more confident, and I knew the direction I would take once I graduated. That was because all cotillion participants were required to declare what their intentions were upon graduating from high school.

I had always been fascinated by hairstyling and how stylists had the ability to transform a person's total image with just a simple cut and style. So I asked a few questions of people in the industry, found a cosmetology school that wasn't too far from home, and made an appointment with the director. Finally, I knew what I was to do. I was feeling pretty good about myself because I had a sense of purpose and direction—or so I thought.

THE UNEXPECTED

"You can make many plans, but the
Lord's purpose will prevail."
—Proverbs 19:21 (NLT)

Sometimes things happen for which we are not prepared. Life has a way of catching us off guard, shaking us at the very core of our existence. Times like these show us what we're really made of. For some, it's an unwanted pregnancy. For others, it's an unexpected injury that robs them of their dream of playing a college sport. For me, it was what happened just two weeks after my graduation.

Around the end of my sophomore year, my dad started complaining of stomach problems, but he refused to go see a doctor. After several months my mom, my sisters and I forced him to see a doctor. Dad had stomach cancer. The last year I spent with him was very sad. He would often share what he was feeling about what he was going through, and we would talk about my future. Dad was too sick to attend the scholarship cotillion or my graduation. Just two weeks after I graduated, my dad passed away.

What should have been a very happy and joyous time of my life ended up being one of the saddest. I had to make a decision about what I was going to do. I just wanted to give up and cry for the rest of my life, but in my heart, I knew that was unacceptable. I wanted Dad to be proud of me, so I prayed and asked God for the strength to carry on. The weeks and months ahead were extremely hard, but by the grace of God, I made it through.

There are times when we can ask God for something, but things don't always turn out the way we hope. During these times, we must forge ahead in faith and trust God for what we do not understand. Even though I didn't feel like I would ever be able to survive losing my dad, or ever stop crying, God had not forgotten me. He still had a plan and a future for me.

So I went off to beauty school and did well. I got my cosmetology license and landed a job in a department store beauty salon. I didn't stop there. I decided to continue my education by enrolling in a community college near home. In the back of my mind, I thought I would one day own my own salon. I was good at what I did and had the clients to prove it. Offers were coming in from all over town. Salon owners wanted me to come and work for them. I couldn't believe it. I had more clients than I could handle. God had truly blessed the work of my hands, but all this would soon change. Little did I know I was about to meet the man I was going to spend the rest of my life with.

Eighteen months later, I graduated college, and the next month, I got married. Life was happening faster than I could have ever imagined. Getting married at twenty-two had certainly not been a part of my plans. I thought I would get married around the age of twenty-six and have a couple of kids by the time I was thirty. But God had something else in mind. He was working out the details of my life according to His divine purpose. My life took an entirely different course than I anticipated.

The year after I got married, I became a mom, and all of my dreams of success took a back seat to the innocent little child

I held in my arms. Her safety and security became my priority. God used that pregnancy to mold me, shape me, mature me, and prepare me for my future. God knows how to use the situations and circumstances of our lives to develop us into who He has destined us to be.

THE PLANS OF THE ENEMY

If you have ever shopped at Target, you've seen their marketing symbol, a red bull's eye. Target wants you to know that whatever you're looking for, you will be on point every time if you shop with them. That's how the enemy sees us. He looks at Christians as though we have a bull's eye on our backs, and he likes to shoot his fiery darts to bring us down. From the day we are born—and perhaps even more from when we are born again—he begins to plan how he will keep us from fulfilling our purpose. No matter what comes your way, don't let anything stop you from discovering and fulfilling your God-given purpose.

Satan may try to use disappointment and discouragement to defeat you if things don't turn out the way you planned. But if you push through those feelings and become determined to do what you were created to do then the enemy won't be able to stop you. First John 3:8 encourages us: "For this purpose the Son of God was manifested, that He might destroy the works of the devil." If God sent Jesus to destroy the works of the devil, then that means that Satan cannot stop you. But you can hinder yourself if you don't push past your obstacles.

> **IF GOD SENT JESUS TO DESTROY THE WORKS OF THE DEVIL, THEN THAT MEANS THAT SATAN CANNOT STOP YOU. BUT YOU CAN HINDER YOURSELF IF YOU DON'T PUSH PAST YOUR OBSTACLES.**

GO FOR IT!

Don't wait another day. Start talking to God about your purpose now. It's easier to go after your dreams when you don't have the responsibility of a spouse and family. Take time and ask God to reveal why He created you and what He has for you to do. Don't stop asking until you discover your purpose. Don't be afraid of what He will reveal because God's plans and purpose for your life will always bring you a sense of joy and fulfillment that you won't find doing anything else. His plans will far outweigh any you may set for yourself. Look for clues—there are signals all around that will help point you in the right direction.

When I became a wife and a mom, my focus shifted from doing what I wanted to do to putting my children before myself. When my children were young, I would dream about someday writing books and becoming an author. I wanted to be able to write fancy, so I would spend time practicing writing my signature. Little did I know I would one day sign thousands of books at my own book signings.

When my daughter was a little girl, she loved to sing with a toy microphone in her hand. She was never afraid to be in front of crowds. In fact, she seemed to come alive, shining brightly whenever she was in front of an audience. She was always great at writing short stories using her vivid imagination. All those things were clues to her purpose: today she is a pastor, speaker, and author.

My son showed his gifts at a young age as well. He seemed to be a natural, born athlete. As soon as he could stand on two legs he was putting the ball into his Little Tikes basketball hoop. From the time he was four, he seemed to understand the game and could dribble down the court when he played organized basketball when he was four years old. My husband noticed his natural ability for the game, so he made sure to steer our son in the direction of his gifts. His gift made room for him, and he earned a full scholarship to play basketball for a Division I university. He went on to play professional basketball in the G-league, NBA Summer League, and in France.

What kind of extracurricular activities are you drawn to?

Where do your natural talents lie?

What comes easy to you? These are questions to ask to help you discover your life's purpose. Start paying closer attention to the clues along the way. Even the personality the Lord has given you is a key factor in discovering what you were created to do. But most importantly ask, ask, and keep on asking. Seek God about your purpose, and keep on seeking—knock and the door will open to you. If you are persistent in prayer, God will reveal your purpose.

You may or may not need to attend college to fulfill your purpose. I don't want to go against what your parents or others may have told you, but depending on what your purpose is, maybe you are to attend a trade school or Bible college. Perhaps you are called to serve your country through one of the branches of the armed forces. Whatever you are purposed to do God will reveal it and order your steps accordingly.

Times have changed. Today, many who have attended college for four or five years are finding themselves unable to get a job in their field. A recent news report told of a young woman who thought she had done everything she was supposed to by attending and graduating from college, only to discover that she could not get a job in her field. She was left with more than $100,000 in student loans to pay back and had to depend on her parents for help with her everyday living expenses. This is not how life is supposed to be, and it's a classic example of why it is important to seek God to know your purpose. God doesn't want you to waste time, energy, or even money, and He doesn't want you to take the long route to get to your purpose.

God cares about you so deeply that He gave me a revelation about your generation through a compelling dream. The dream reminds me of a story in the Bible story which tells of the prophet Ezekiel who had a divine encounter with the Lord. The Spirit of the Lord took him and sat him in the midst of a valley full of dead men's bones. Ezekiel passed all around the bones to capture a realistic view of the situation before God began to speak to him and tell him what to do about it. You can read the full story in Ezekiel 37. In Ezekiel's case, the dry bones represented the whole nation of Israel who had lost their hope. However, the bodies in my dream represent today's youth.

A DIVINELY INSPIRED DREAM

I found myself in a large field much like a cemetery. It was full of what appeared to be dead bodies lying in open graves. Just imagine how creepy it would feel to visit your local cemetery and instead of seeing headstones or grave markers, you saw open graves holding individual bodies. The experience left me feeling uneasy, apprehensive, and frozen in my place. I wanted to run, yet I knew I didn't have to be afraid because the Lord was with me. He wanted to show me something significant.

The Lord spoke to my heart and told me to walk around the graves, and not only that, at one point He instructed me to stop and take a closer look at young people who were lying in the graves. What I found unique about the situation is what I witnessed. As I looked more intently, I saw signs of life. There was a slight twitch of the eye of one individual. There was a wiggle of a finger with another individual. I was shocked! These signs of life signified that although the bodies were buried, there was still hope. Then the Holy Spirit spoke to my heart again, and this time, He told me speak life into those who originally appeared dead, commanding them to rise to a new life.

I believe God wanted me to write this book as a lifeline to offer hope, encouragement, and life to those who are weary and feel like giving up. So hang on. God has more in store that reaches far beyond your current circumstance.

> HANG ON. GOD HAS MORE IN STORE THAT REACHES FAR BEYOND YOUR CURRENT CIRCUMSTANCE.

May the words of this book strengthen, reinforce, and empower you to keep pressing on. God has a future for you filled with hope.

COME CLOSER!

God knows why He created you. He wants you to come to Him to know your purpose.

What are some things that come naturally to you? What is God speaking to your heart?

_____

_____

_____

_____

_____

_____

_____

_____

_____

_____

_____

_____

Prayer: "Father, You alone know why You created me. I ask You to show me what my purpose is and give me a vision for my future. Help me to make the right decisions that will lead me to my purpose."

CHAPTER EIGHT

COME AND FILL UP

"Jesus said to them, 'Come and eat breakfast.'"
—John 21:12

Can you believe it? Jesus, the Son of God, cooked breakfast! I can only imagine how delicious the food must have tasted, how it was cooked with such love and compassion for His followers. You see, God cares about your spiritual and natural food. After His resurrection, Jesus appeared to His disciples on a few different occasions. One of those times was when Peter and some of the others had been fishing all night but didn't catch a single fish. The following morning Jesus was on the shore and yelled out to the men in the boat. He asked if they had caught anything. When they replied no, Jesus instructed them on how to catch some fish. Peter and the boys did what Jesus said and they caught 153 big fish—more than enough.

A few years ago while looking for something decent to watch on television, I came across a fascinating show called *Deadliest Catch* on the Discovery Channel. Aside from the amazing cinematography which offered an up-close view of the ships rocking on the tumultuous waves of the sea at night, what drew my attention was the complexities in the lives of modern-day fishermen. As I watched the show each week, I began to think about Peter and other disciples who were professional fishermen. God revealed something powerful as I watched the men on the reality show count the number of fish or crabs they caught on each expedition. If they had a big catch, the men roared with excitement, but when they caught little to nothing, they felt defeated. Why? Because the size of the catch represented the amount of money each man would earn to take back to his family. Fishing was their livelihood.

When Peter and the other disciples did what Jesus told them to do, they caught such an abundance of fish that they could barely pull in the net, but that wasn't all. We read in John 21:9-10: "Then, as soon as they had come to land, they saw a fire of coals there and fish laid on it, and bread." While the disciples were out struggling to catch fish, Jesus had already prepared a meal. This story shows us Jesus understands our struggles and cares about every aspect of our lives. He cared enough to cook breakfast for His boys knowing they were hungry, but He also used the opportunity to teach Peter the importance of feeding the lambs (new believers) and the sheep (mature believers). Because while it's important to feed the body, it's just as important to feed the spirit. Our physical bodies hunger for natural food, while our spirits hunger for spiritual food. We need both. Natural food cannot satisfy our need for spiritual food.

> OUR PHYSICAL BODIES HUNGER FOR NATURAL FOOD, WHILE OUR SPIRITS HUNGER FOR SPIRITUAL FOOD. WE NEED BOTH. NATURAL FOOD CANNOT SATISFY OUR NEED FOR SPIRITUAL FOOD.

SPIRITUAL FOOD

"I am the bread of life. He who comes to Me shall never hunger, and he who believes in Me shall never thirst."
—John 6:35

Have you ever had a taste for something but didn't really know what you wanted? Sometimes, I'll start eating different things but nothing seems to really hit the spot because what I'm feeling is deeper than a physical hunger. When our spirits are hungry it is a lot like being physically hungry. When we don't know what we really want or need, we can try to fill ourselves up with other things instead of turning to God and allowing Him to fill us.

When we're empty inside we have a tendency to look to outward things to satisfy our inner longings. We've all felt it—longing for fulfillment and satisfaction. Some people try to fill up on food, like I've done at times. Some use extreme exercise, some shop excessively, some use sex, and some drugs or alcohol. But the emptiness doesn't go away until we turn to God because everything we need is in Him. He is the sustainer of life, the only true source of spiritual fulfillment.

Jesus understands our physical need for food and nourishment. When the crowds gathered to listen to Him teach, He was moved with compassion because they had traveled from afar and had sat for long periods of time. On one occasion a boy gave his lunch to Jesus, and He fed five thousand people with it. Now that's a miracle: when we give the little that we have to God, He turns it into much. After Jesus performed this miracle the people realized that He truly was the Prophet who had come into the world. When Jesus left to meet up with His disciples who had traveled to Capernaum, the people were looking for Him. But for what reason:

> Jesus answered, "I tell you for certain that you are not looking for me because you saw the miracles, but because you ate all the food you wanted. Don't work for food that spoils. Work for food that gives eternal life. The Son of Man will give you this food."
> —John 6:26-27 (CEV)

As the people continued to talk to Jesus to find out how He was able to do miracles, He told them to just believe in Him, whom God had sent. But they still wanted Jesus to perform some sort of sign so that they could believe in Him:

> Jesus then told them, "I tell you for certain that Moses wasn't the one who gave you bread from heaven. My Father is the One Who gives you the

true bread from heaven. And the bread that God gives is the one who came down from heaven to give life to the world."

The people said, "Sir, give us this bread and don't ever stop!" Jesus replied, "I am the bread that gives life! No one who comes to me will ever be hungry. No one who has faith in me will ever be thirsty."
—Matthew 6:32-35 (CEV).

Jesus calls Himself the bread of life because He came down from heaven and gave life to a world full of people who were dead in their trespasses and sins. When we believe in Jesus and accept Him as our Lord and the Savior of our lives, we have everything we need to experience true fulfillment. But when we don't spend time developing our relationship with our heavenly Father, we end up going back to the world.

> WHEN WE BELIEVE IN JESUS AND ACCEPT HIM AS THE LORD AND SAVIOR OF OUR LIVES, WE HAVE EVERYTHING WE NEED TO EXPERIENCE TRUE FULFILLMENT.

Somehow we must think the world has something more fun, exciting, or more fulfilling to offer. But when the world treats us cruelly and we get hurt and messed-up out there, we turn back to the One who truly loves us unconditionally. After all we've done, after turning our backs on Him, God is still there waiting on us with outstretched arms saying, "Come!" He never leaves us or forsakes us. And when we come back to God He never rejects us because He's faithful to us even when we're not faithful to Him.

JESUS IS THE WORD AND BREAD OF LIFE

"And the Word became flesh and dwelt among us,
and we beheld His glory, the glory as of the only
begotten of the Father, full of grace and truth."
—John 1:14

The Bible says that Jesus *is* the Word. Since Jesus *is* the Word, then we need to partake of the Word as our daily bread.

As you spend more time in prayer and in the Word, you will start to discover that the feelings and longings for other things begin to fade away, and your desire for Him begins to increase. Nothing can be compared to the rich fellowship of God's presence. It's addictive! It is so satisfying that once you have experienced it, you won't want to live without it.

Prayer and the Word will become the best part of your day because there is fullness of joy in the presence of the Lord. Through daily prayer, God will fill you to overflowing with the kind of peace and joy that you can't get anywhere else. If you attempt to fill up on anything other than God, you will always be left feeling empty and needing something more. It's like being physically hungry and trying to fill up on junk food which has no nutritional value. Your body will be left longing for some real food to give it nourishment.

When you know the difference between natural and spiritual hunger, you can start paying attention to feelings of dissatisfaction, loneliness, or emptiness. When you feel that way, check to see if you have gotten lax with spending time with God and reading your Bible. You will likely discover that's where those feelings are coming from. This usually doesn't happen because we blatantly decide to stop spending time with God or reading the Word, but it happens very subtly, little by little, as we get busy and distracted doing other things.

COME CLOSER!

Only God can fill the empty places inside your heart.

Do you feel empty inside? Do you struggle with feelings of dissatisfaction? What is God speaking to you through this chapter?

_____

_____

_____

_____

_____

_____

_____

_____

_____

_____

_____

_____

Prayer: "Father God, I release every pain and disappointment of my life, and I ask You to fill me to overflowing with Your love, peace, and joy."

CHAPTER NINE

A WAKE-UP CALL

*"Listen! I am standing and knocking at your
door. If you hear my voice and open the door,
I will come in and we will eat together."*
—Revelation 3:20 (CEV)

One afternoon while taking a short nap, I was suddenly awakened by a loud knock. It was the kind of persistent knocking that tells you the person is not going to go away easily. It startled me because I couldn't imagine who would be knocking so hard; I wasn't expecting anyone. I jumped up and went to the front door, only to discover that no one was there.

I instantly had the awareness that the knocking I had heard was actually the Lord knocking loudly and persistently at the door of my heart. Why did I have this experience? It was because God wanted to spend time with me. This wasn't a single occurrence—it has happened three or four times over the years. Each time it was during seasons of prayerlessness, when I wasn't consistently spending time with God. I had allowed other things to creep in and override my priority of spending time in prayer.

When God desperately wants to spend time with us, He will persistently knock at the door of our hearts to draw us to Him. How we respond is up to us. If we hear His voice and open the door to Him, He has promised to come in and dine with us and we with Him. Wow! How would you like to sit down at a meal and have God's undivided attention and ear and actually have a conversation with Him? That's what prayer is. We have the awesome privilege of experiencing this kind of sweet fellowship whenever we desire, as we spend time with Him in prayer. When was the last time you spent quality time alone with God? Is He knocking at the door of your heart now, trying to get you to let Him in?

If two people are going to sit down together over a meal that means either they have a good relationship with each other, or they hope to establish one. I've never sat down to eat with an enemy before, have you? Having a meal with Jesus would be captivating. Engaging in a conversation over a meal, nothing could get more intimate or personal than that. If you open your heart to the Lord, not just one time at the point of salvation, but daily, it will transform your entire life. Daily fellowship with the Lord is the lifeline of your Christian walk. You will grow and develop into a strong mature believer.

WATCH AND PRAY

"Therefore humble yourselves under the mighty hand
of God, that He may exalt you in due time, casting
all your care upon Him, for He cares for you. Be sober;

be vigilant; because your adversary walks about like
a roaring lion, seeking whom he may devour."
—1 Peter 5:6-8

One time when I was sitting at my desk praying, I suddenly had a vision. A vision is like a dream except you're awake. I saw a giant lying stretched out on a couch, fast asleep. He was snoring away, without a care in the world. He wasn't concerned about anyone bothering him because of his enormous size. Who would dare harm him? But while he was sleeping, an army of small imps quietly marched in and tied up the giant's hands and feet. They bound him tightly so that he couldn't move. By the time the giant began to wake up and realize what was going on, it was too late to do anything. He was utterly helpless.

When it comes to spiritual things, are you sleeping or are you awake? When you're spiritually awake you are alert, watching and praying. But if you are asleep, life can catch you by surprise. God wants you to be spiritually awake so that the enemy won't be able to sneak up on you and catch you off guard.

The giant I saw represents the church. I don't mean a building where we meet. The church is you and me and every member of the body of Christ, individually and collectively. When we are spiritually asleep, we are not alert. We are not spending time in prayer and the Word of God. This is the only way the devil can sneak up on us with surprise attacks.

God wants us to take our relationship with Him seriously. We do that by coming to Him on a daily basis. The devil is always searching for opportunities or open doors to execute his plan of destruction in our lives, so we need to stay on top of our game and keep him in his place. Prayerlessness is a form of pride. When we don't pray, we're really saying we don't have time for God, or we don't need God in our lives. We think we can do life all by ourselves—until things go terribly wrong. It takes humility to depend on God and rely on Him for help. Having a relationship with God makes us strong Christians who are able to resist the devil and keep him out of our lives.

> IT TAKES HUMILITY TO DEPEND ON GOD AND RELY ON HIM FOR HELP. HAVING A RELATIONSHIP WITH GOD MAKES US STRONG CHRISTIANS WHO ARE ABLE TO RESIST THE DEVIL AND KEEP HIM OUT OF OUR LIVES.

"God is strong, and He wants you to be strong. So take everything the Master has set out for you, well-made weapons of the best materials. And put them to use so you will be able to stand up to everything the devil throws your way. This is no afternoon athletic contest that we'll walk away from and forget about in a couple of hours. This is for keeps, a life-or-death fight to the finish against the devil and his angels."
—Ephesians 6:10-12 (MSG)

"Be prepared. You're up against far more than you can handle on your own. Take all the help you can get, every weapon God has issued, so that when it's all over but the shouting you'll still be on your feet. Trust, righteousness, peace, faith, and salvation are more than words. Learn how to apply them. You'll need them throughout your life. God's Word is an indispensable weapon. In the same way, prayer is essential in the ongoing warfare. Pray hard and long. Pray for your brothers and sisters. Keep your eyes open. Keep each other's spirits up so that no one falls behind or drops out."
—Ephesians 6:13-18 (MSG)

From the moment we give our hearts to the Lord, as Christians we are delivered from the power of darkness into the kingdom of His Son of love. Therefore, Satan, the god of this world, desires to kill, steal, and destroy, to make things as difficult for us as he possibly can.

We are in a fight!

Will we stay with God, or will we turn away from Him?

Will we succumb to the pressures of worldly temptations, or will we walk in the Spirit and in obedience to God's Word?

Will we fulfill the purpose God has for our lives, or will we go our own way? We need God like never before!

The choice is ours. We can push Him aside and treat Him as if He's unimportant, or we can come to Him and cultivate a real relationship with Him. God never forces us to spend time with Him. He is gentle and patient and kind. What are you going to do? The choice is yours.

COME CLOSER!

When we don't spend enough time with God, He will knock at the door of our hearts.

Has God been trying to get your attention? Have you been sensing Him drawing you closer to Him? What is God speaking to you through this chapter?

_____

_____

_____

_____

_____

_____

_____

_____

_____

_____

_____

_____

Prayer: "Heavenly Father, I repent for not spending more time with You. I ask You to stir me up to pray more and give me the discipline I need to be consistent."

CHAPTER TEN

COME TO THE LIGHT

"The light has come into the world, and people who do evil things are judged guilty because they love the dark more than the light. People who do evil hate the light and won't come to the light because it clearly shows what they have done. But everyone who lives by the truth will come to the light because they want others to know that God is really the one doing what they do."
—John 3:19-21 (CEV)

The world is a dark place. Its systems are designed to pull you into the darkness. Most of the music, books, and movies that are geared toward today's youth are designed to appeal to the flesh, not the spirit because the enemy's plan is to draw you into his kingdom using things that look good to your eyes, and feel good to your body. He wants you to believe if you do what the world does, you can have what the world has: money, fame, and success. The devil knows how to lure you into his way of doing things, never mentioning that his path really leads to destruction. But God's path leads to life. Everything about God is light and bright.

When we live in sin we like being in dark places so that what we're doing won't be exposed. But God still sees. When we're walking with God, we love the light because we are living a life that represents the kingdom of God. Jesus said, "I am the light of the world. He who follows Me shall not walk in darkness, but have the light of life" (John 8:12). The apostle Paul wrote, "For you were once darkness, but now you are light in the Lord. Walk as children of light" (Ephesians 5:8). And 1 Thessalonians 5:5 says, "You are all sons of light and sons of the day. We are not of the night nor of darkness." So as Christians, Christ followers, we should have no part of darkness. Our whole lives should represent light and life, so that everywhere we go people in darkness are drawn to His light shining in and through us.

> SO AS CHRISTIANS, CHRIST FOLLOWERS, WE SHOULD HAVE NO PART OF DARKNESS. OUR WHOLE LIVES SHOULD REPRESENT LIGHT AND LIFE, SO THAT EVERYWHERE WE GO PEOPLE IN DARKNESS ARE DRAWN TO HIS LIGHT SHINING IN AND THROUGH US.

God gave His Son to save us from our sins. He showed just how much He loves us by reaching out to us even when we were in darkness. We were dead in our trespasses and sins, yet God accepted us into the kingdom of light. Our sinful condition didn't matter to God at all; He still wanted us. Jesus came down from heaven into a dark world. If Jesus was willing to come to us, why wouldn't we want to come to Him?

"He has delivered us from the power of darkness and conveyed us into the kingdom of the Son of His love."
—Colossians 1:13

Jesus came to you when He came to earth to save you; now it is your turn to come to Him. You have to choose God's light over the devil's darkness. It is a day-by-day, hour-by-hour choice. I won't tell you it's going to be easy because it's not. You have to be deliberate about spending time with God because you're in a fight. You have to approach life like a fighter, not like someone who is weak.

Bullies like to pick on weak, timid, and fearful people because they're easy targets, and that's all the devil is—a bully. But he has no power or authority over you. He can't make you do anything that you don't want to do. All he can do is lie to you, and try to entice you with the things of this world. If you want to walk in the light, you have to walk in the Spirit by walking in the Word of God. And you must stay close to God by spending time with Him every day.

COME CLOSER!

When you turn away from the things of the world and turn to God, you are choosing light over darkness, good over bad.

Does your world seem light or dark? Are you struggling with any hidden or secret sins that nobody knows about? What is God speaking to your heart through this chapter?

_____

_____

_____

_____

_____

_____

_____

_____

_____

_____

_____

_____

Prayer: "Father God, please shine Your light on any dark areas in my life. Help me to make right choices, and chase away all fear!"

CHAPTER ELEVEN

CHOOSE LIFE

"I call heaven and earth as witnesses today against
you, that I have set before you life and death,
blessing and cursing; therefore choose life, that
both you and your descendants may live."
—Deuteronomy 30:19

From the day we are born, we are pulled in two directions. There are two plans for our lives, two different paths we can follow. One path is God's path for our lives, and the other path is the devil's. One path leads to life, the other to death. God has blessed us with a free will to choose which path we will take.

I was born and raised in a Christian home. I accepted Jesus as my Lord and Savior when I was ten years old. So, from an early age, I wanted to do the right thing and be a good person. I loved God and wanted to please Him, but I was unaware that there was another force out there pulling me in another direction. Had I known, I would have clung to God with all my might.

> ## THERE IS PRESSURE TO BE ACCEPTED BY THOSE AROUND YOU, AND WHO DOESN'T WANT TO FIT IN?

Teenagers are faced with a multitude of decisions and choices, with corresponding consequences. There is pressure to be accepted by those around you, and who doesn't want to fit in? You are discovering who you are and what you want out of life. During this pivotal time in life it is important to it stay close to God. He will navigate you safely through to the place He has planned.

> *"Enter through the narrow gate; for wide is the gate*
> *and spacious and broad is the way that leads away*
> *to destruction, and many are those who are entering*
> *through it. But the gate is narrow (contracted by*
> *pressure) and the way is straightened and compressed*
> *that leads away to life, and few are those who find it."*
> —Matthew 7:13-14 (AMP)

God has plainly told us which choice to make in life. He's not trying to trick us, nor does He leave us to figure out everything on our own. But He has told us that the doorway leading to life is a narrow and difficult one. So before we ever choose to follow God, we must realize that things won't always be easy or trouble-free. But we can rest assured that, no matter what we encounter on our journey, God will be with us.

Satan, on the other hand, tries to make his path seem fun, easy, and free. But it's all just an illusion. In reality, to go down his path is very costly, and the price is much higher than anyone would ever want to pay. The devil is a thief and a trickster who promises one thing and delivers another. His path is wide so that many can fit on it together. His path leads to nothing but heartache and destruction—even death. Because his primary function is to steal, kill, and destroy us, he works overtime to figure out ways to cause us to miss our destination, the very purpose for our existence.

It wasn't until I became an adult that I could look back and see how he strategically entered my life by putting certain people in my pathway to trip me up and cause me to stumble. Satan uses subtle things to lure us astray. Listening to the wrong kind of music was one entry point that gave him access to my mind and subtly lured me away from my relationship with God. I listened to love songs that served to do nothing but make me lonely. The devil tried so hard to get me off course, and sometimes he was successful. And whenever I made wrong choices, I was always sorry. In my heart, I knew I belonged to God, and I was always striving to get back into fellowship with Him.

CHOOSING YOUR PATH

"Come now, and let us reason together, says the Lord. Though your sins are like scarlet, they shall be as

white as snow; though they are red like crimson,
they shall be like wool. If you are willing and
obedient, you shall eat the good of the land; But if
you refuse and rebel, you will be devoured by the
sword. For the mouth of the Lord has spoken it."
—Isaiah 1:18-20 (AMP)

John's Story

One of my brothers passed away when he was a baby, leaving my brother John surrounded by girls. He was desperately hoping for another brother. When my mother returned home from the hospital holding me in her arms, she went right over to him and said, "Here, boy, this is the best I could do." John took me into his arms and the rest is history; we had a very special relationship from that day forward.

John had a rough life. He always seemed to be in trouble. He made a habit of breaking the rules. He seemed to gravitate toward the wrong people, and they always seemed to do the wrong things. John ended up dropping out of high school, and eventually went to prison for a few years. For more than half of his life, John chose the wrong path.

I never stopped praying for him to turn his life around and choose the path that leads to life. I knew God could do it and would do it if I prayed. My mom never gave up on her son either. One day she felt strongly that something bad was going to happen to John if he didn't turn around. By this time he was an adult, living in another state. He was leaving work late one night, when he was shot down in the back of an alley and left to die. In that moment he cried out to God, "Lord save me!

Don't let me die here like a dog." God heard John's cries on that dark night. I believe God allowed the accident to happen to get John's attention—He goes to great lengths to get us to come back to Him.

The shooting left John paralyzed from the waist down. I wish that the incident had never happened, but because of it, John's life was never the same. He became a new creation in Christ. He loved God with all of his heart, and he spent the remainder of his days preaching the gospel right from his wheelchair. John had ten years to shine his light for God before he passed away from complications due to his injuries.

God's plan is for you to live a long and abundant life that overflows with blessings, but if you choose the wrong path there will be corresponding consequences. And, believe it or not, those consequences can and probably will affect your children and even grandchildren. That's how sin works. It's passed down through the generations.

"All whom my Father gives [entrust] to Me will come
to Me; and the one who comes to Me [I will never,
no never, reject one of them who comes to Me]."
—John 6:37 (AMP)

If you've been caught up in a series of bad choices, it's only because Satan lured you down his path by using something that appealed to your senses. But at any time you can make a decision to choose God's path for your life. God is always waiting with open arms when we come back to Him. All it takes is having a desire to change, and making a firm decision to do so. If you cry out to God from a sincere heart, He will hear you and help you. He will never turn you away.

> GOD IS ALWAYS WAITING WITH OPEN ARMS WHEN WE COME BACK TO HIM. ALL IT TAKES IS HAVING A DESIRE TO CHANGE AND MAKING A FIRM DECISION TO DO SO.
> IF YOU CRY OUT TO GOD FROM A SINCERE HEART, HE WILL HEAR YOU AND HELP YOU. HE WILL NEVER TURN YOU AWAY.

THE FATHER'S HEART

Jesus told a story that really reveals God's heart towards His children. You may have heard it before, but may not realize why Jesus shared the story of the prodigal son. I believe it was because He knew there would be times when we would walk away from God and need to be restored to right fellowship. And because He wanted us to understand that, no matter what we've done, God will always welcome us home with His arms wide open, full of love and compassion.

This is how the story goes in Luke 15:

Once a man had two sons. The younger son said to his father, "Give me my share of the property." So the father divided his property between his two sons.

Not long after that, the younger son packed up everything he owned and left for a foreign country, where he wasted all his money in wild living. He had spent everything, when a bad famine spread through that whole land. Soon he had nothing to eat.

He went to work for a man in that country, and the man sent him out to take care of his pigs. He would have been glad to eat what the pigs were eating, but no one gave him a thing.

Finally, he came to his senses and said, "My father's workers have plenty to eat, and here I am, starving to death! I will go to my father and say to him, 'Father, I have sinned against God in heaven and against you. I am no longer good enough to be called your son. Treat me like one of your workers.'"

The younger son got up and started back to his father. But when he was still a long way off, his father saw him and felt sorry for him. He ran to his son and hugged and kissed him.

The son said, "Father, I have sinned against God in heaven and against you. I am no longer good enough to be called your son."

But his father said to the servants, "Hurry and bring the best clothes and put them on him. Give him a ring for his finger and sandals for his feet. Get the best calf and prepare it, so we can eat and celebrate. This son of mine was dead, but has now come back to life. He was lost and has now been found." And they began to celebrate. —vv. 11-24 (CEV)

If you have been doing things you shouldn't and have somehow gotten away from God, He has nothing but love waiting for you. Don't ever believe the lies of the enemy when he tells you that you have messed up too bad to turn back now. Just as the father in this story greeted his son with rejoicing and gave him gifts and a special celebration, God will greet you the same way. It is never too late to choose life.

> ## IT IS NEVER TOO LATE TO CHOOSE LIFE.

The young man in this story had a rich dad. For whatever reason, he wasn't satisfied at home, so he asked for his inheritance and left. When he got out in the world, he had a good time living wild, partying and spending his money. But when it ran out he had to resort to eating like pigs in a pigpen. He was living like a homeless person, with no food or money. There were three things that the prodigal son did in order for his life to be restored to the way it used to be.

If you need to get back on track, you might follow his three steps:

1) He came to his senses—realizing that his dad's hired servants were living a better life than he was.
2) He made a decision to go back home—thinking about what he would say when he went back home to his father.
3) He humbled himself—confessing his sins and asking to be restored back into the family.

The father had been waiting on his son with great expectation because he knew one day he would come back home. When he saw his son coming towards the house from far off in the distance, he started planning a big celebration. When we are away from God, we're in a backslidden state. That means we've gone back to our old life before we accepted the Lord. We may have fun doing whatever we've chosen to do, but that pleasure only lasts for a season. At some point, we have to come to our senses and see how terrible life is without God and how much better it is with God.

From the moment we make up our mind to go back to God, there is rejoicing in heaven. Just as the father greeted his son with rejoicing and gave him a party, a ring, and a robe—which signified that he was restored back to the way things were before—God will completely restore us back to His family, with all the blessings and benefits that come with it.

COME CLOSER!

When you choose God's path, you choose LIFE. When you choose the enemy's path, you choose DEATH.

Take a look at the path you're on. What do you see? Is the path you're on leading you to life or to death? What is God speaking to you through this chapter?

_____

_____

_____

_____

_____

_____

_____

_____

_____

_____

_____

Prayer: "Heavenly Father, help me to choose the path of life and stay on it. Give me strength on the journey, and if I start to wander astray, please put me back on course."

CHAPTER TWELVE

"LAST CALL!"

*"God loved the people of this world so much that He
gave His only Son, so that everyone who has faith in
Him will have eternal life and never really die."*
—John 3:16 (CEV)

Love is what sent Jesus to earth. Love is what put Him on the
cross. And love is what will bring Him back to earth again.
After Jesus fulfilled His purpose on earth, to destroy the works
of the devil by shedding His innocent blood on the cross, He
spent a short time with His disciples until it was time to return
to heaven. Acts 1:9-11 tells us what happened when Jesus was
giving them their final instructions:

> *Now when He had spoken this things, while they
> watched, He was taken up, and a cloud received
> Him out of their sight. And while they looked stead-
> fast toward heaven as He went up, behold two men
> stood by them in white apparel, who also said,
> "Men of Galilee, why do you stand gazing up into*

heaven? This same Jesus, who was taken up from
you into heaven will so come in like manner as you
saw Him go into heaven."

Today, Jesus sits at God's right hand praying for those of us here on earth. One day, God will send Jesus back to earth the way He ascended into the clouds. Only, this time, He will take us back with Him. Jesus talked to His disciples about the events that would take place in the last days before His return. Although the disciples wanted to know the precise timing the events would happen, Jesus responded, "No one knows the day or hour when these things will happen, not even the angels in heaven or the Son himself. Only the Father knows" (Matthew 24:36, NLT). There are two important points to consider from this passage. First, Jesus could not tell His disciples information He did not know. Second, Jesus wants us to be ready at all times, whenever He returns.

In 1 Thessalonians 5:1-11, the apostle Paul wrote the following:
But concerning the times and the seasons, brethren,
you have no need that I should write to you. For you
yourselves know perfectly that the day of the Lord
so comes as a thief in the night. For when they say,
"Peace and safety!" then sudden destruction comes
upon them, as labor pains upon a pregnant woman.
And they shall not escape. But you, brethren are
not in darkness, so that this Day should overtake
you as a thief. You are all sons of light and sons
of the day. We are not of the night or of darkness.
Therefore let us not sleep, as others do, but let us
watch and be sober. For those who sleep, sleep at

night, and those who get drunk are drunk at night. But let us who are of the day be sober, putting on the breastplate of faith and love, and as a helmet the hope of salvation. For God did not appoint us to wrath, but to obtain salvation through our Lord Jesus Christ, who died for us, that whether we wake or sleep, we should live together with Him. Therefore comfort each other and edify one another, just as you also are doing.

Paul sums it up so well. If we want to go with Jesus, we need to be ready when He comes. We must live a life that is pleasing to God and let go of all sin. Instead of going after what we want, we must go after what God wants by doing the will of God and fulfilling our purposes. Our time on earth is just a short period of time in the light of eternity. Now is the time to get to know the One with whom we will spend all eternity. If we have no relationship with Him, how can we expect to be ready?

> **GOD WAS REACHING OUT TO US WHEN HE SENT JESUS, BUT NOW IT'S OUR TURN TO REACH OUT TO HIM BY RESPONDING TO HIS INVITATION TO COME.**

God was reaching out to us when He sent Jesus, but now it's our turn to reach out to Him by responding to His invitation to come. It takes moving away from worldly things to spend time with Him in the secret place. God has allowed us time to master the love-walk. When we learn to love God and love each other we have fulfilled God's greatest commandment. We learn all about love by spending time with God, the source of all love! Revelation is the last book in the Bible. It is the message or prophecy that God revealed to John concerning the things to take place before Jesus returns to earth. Many Christians struggle with the symbolism used in Revelation, so they avoid reading it altogether. But John said many things: "Blessed is he who reads and those who hear the words of this prophecy, and keep those things which are written in it; for the time is near" (Revelation 1:3). Pay close attention to Jesus's final words in the last chapter:

"Behold, I am coming quickly! Blessed is he who keeps the words of the prophecy of this book. . . . And behold, I am coming quickly, and My reward is with Me, to give to every one according to his work."
—Revelation 22:7 and 12

"Blessed are those who do His commandments, that they may have the right to the tree of life, and may enter through the gates into the city. But outside are dogs and sorcerers and sexually immoral and murderers and idolaters, and whoever loves and practices a lie. . . . And the Spirit and the bride say, 'Come!' And let him who hears say, 'Come!' And let him who thirsts come. Whoever desires, let him take the water of life freely."
—Revelation 22:14-15 and 17

"He who testifies to these things says, 'Surely I am coming quickly.' Amen. Even so, come, Lord Jesus! The grace of our Lord Jesus Christ be with you all. Amen."
—Revelation 22:21

This should be the cry of every believer in Christ: "Come, Lord Jesus!" The world can only offer us darkness. And as things get worse on earth, we will long to be with God in heaven, where there is no darkness: "There shall be no night there; They need no lamp nor light of the sun, for the Lord God gives them light. And they shall reign forever and ever" (Revelation 22:5).

These scriptures are not meant to put fear in your heart about the end of the world but to awaken you to the truth of the Word of God. God loves you so much that He wants to spend time with you now and throughout eternity. God is calling you. Will you come?

> **TO KNOW GOD IS TO LOVE HIM. TO LOVE GOD IS TO DO HIS WILL AND OBEY HIS COMMANDS.**

To know God is to love Him. To love God is to do His will and obey His commands.

It's not enough to say we are Christians or that we love God. Our actions should correspond with our beliefs and the profession of our faith in Christ. Jesus warned, "Not everyone who calls out to me, 'Lord! Lord!' will enter the kingdom of Heaven. Only those who actually do the will of my Father in heaven will enter" (Matthew 7:21). It's that simple. The choice is yours.

COME CLOSER!

Jesus came to you, so you could come to Him. One day, He will come again.

If Jesus were to come back today, would you be ready? What are some things that may be keeping you from being ready for Jesus's return? What is God speaking to you through this chapter?

_____

_____

_____

_____

_____

_____

_____

_____

_____

_____

_____

_____

Prayer: "Father God, help me to be ready when Jesus comes back again. Help me to let go of any relationships, habits, or sin that stands in the way of my relationship with You."

TEEN RESOURCES

For additional help or support contact one of the following

For teen counseling online:

BetterHelp.com

Mycounselor.online.com

Mytalkspace.com

For suicidal thoughts:

Call or text 988-24 hours a day 7 days a week

Go to 988lifeline.org or call or text 988

TITLES BY
KATHY R. GREEN

Pray-ers Bear Fruit:
Become a Person of Prayer

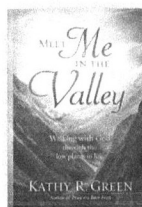

Meet Me in the Valley: Walking With God
Through the Low Places in Life

TO CONTACT
THE AUTHOR

For more information...
Contact Kathy by visiting KathyRGreen.com.
Kathy would love to hear from you. Please feel free to send her
your prayer request or testimony of how this book has made
a difference in your life.

@KathyRGreen